IT TAKES TWO,

GOD

AND

YOU

Keep Looking Up

DON W. ROBERTSON

WESTBOW
PRESS®
A DIVISION OF THOMAS NELSON
& ZONDERVAN

WestBow Press books may be ordered through booksellers or by contacting:

WestBow Press
A Division of Thomas Nelson & Zondervan
1663 Liberty Drive
Bloomington, IN 47403
www.westbowpress.com
844-714-3454

Holy Bible, New International Version®, NIV® Copyright ©1973, 1978, 1984,
2011 by Biblica, Inc.® Used by permission. All rights reserved worldwide.

ISBN: 979-8-3850-3278-5 (sc)
ISBN: 979-8-3850-3279-2 (hc)
ISBN: 979-8-3850-3280-8 (e)

Library of Congress Control Number: 2024918331

Print information available on the last page.

WestBow Press rev. date: 01/25/2025

CONTENTS

MY LOVE ONES

My deceased first wife, Doris M. Robertson (1940-1993)

My deceased second wife, Nancy M. Robertson (1935-2011)

My deceased oldest son, Don W. Robertson (1962-2009)

My son, Brad S. Robertson and his wife, Teresa

My dearest daughter, Loretta E. Robertson

My family and friends

My friends at Cookeville Nazarene Church-First Church United Pentecostal

My friends at Maysville Community Church

My special friends of Cookeville Pacesetters

My friends of Heritage Pointe Senior Living Community

The American military and veterans

INTRODUCTION

The first fifty-five years of my life journey over ninety years, my love for my Lord Jesus Christ has grown greater and stronger each year. By serving Him being more gentle and kinder in Christian love for my country, my church family, my family and my friends. God has bless me over the years with my faithful deceased first wife with an outstanding marriage of thirty-two years with our three children, consisting two faithful sons and a faithful lovely daughter. Our oldest son is also deceased, died after Christmas 2009. Like most families during those years, I was in my working years as an accountant with Dana Corporation for we were living on my income taken care of my wife and our three children. Again being bless with twelve wonderful marriage years with my faithful deceased second wife with her faithful, kind, and outstanding family. During those wonderful times we were both in our retirement years having both financial means and good health with time seeing our family and friends in other states. Those wonderful years we travel the good ole USA, both the southeastern and southwestern parts of Canada, five countries of Europe, Ireland, and Scotland. Most happy made those world trips with my an a wife years ago, it was a wonderful experience both of us.

The last twenty-five years I have enjoyed reading and study Bible prophecy. I believed more than ever that we are living in the end times or the last days of this church age. For each day I can feel it, I can hear it, and I can see it of the near coming Rapture. Always keep looking up, always be ready, and always be watching for our Lord coming soon Christians-belivers. That is the time when our Lord Jesus be coming in the air for His Church for those faithful born again Brothers and Sisters in Christ being caught up for that life time journey into the Heaven of all heaven.

We can see all these end times happenings today and all the tomorrows yet to come by using the internet or smart phones, reading your daily newspaper, hearing the local, state, national, and world news on the radio or seeing those end times come alive by TV. What will happen to our America and the rest the whole wide world into the future years to come? For the real truthful answers, just read and study your Bible each day for the only true answers or facts what the people of this world will be facing during their life's journey. Prepare yourself by being more faithful for your salvation that you be living in the Heaven of all heavens with our Heavenly Father and our Lord Jesus or be living in the burning fire of hell with Satan the devil. Study God's Words in your Bible for it will give you the blessing answers for the following four W's: the what's, the when's, the where's, and the why's. We know for sure that our Heavenly Father and His Son, our Jesus Christ has all the real true answers.

We are seeing deteriorating Christian morals and ethical values in our beloved America. After many years of reckless borrowing and spending, America's debt level is at complete breaking point. The national debt including large annual interest will never be debt paid under any future American political leadership or by the taxpayers.

During the twenty-first century it's hard believe what is happening in this world, there is so much hatred for God's

Church, all Christians in our America, and those faithful people in other world countries. Is our Heavenly Father telling our America this is the "wake-up call" regarding the morals and sins of our country? This newer chapter for my "ninety golden years" life journey receiving a blessing calling from my Heavenly Father for me to write these two books. My Lord Jesus gave me the words with Bible verses to write. I am using the HIV Study Bible of New International Version through out this book. Since we are living in evil and sinful trouble times of this new twenty-first century, there is a greater need for a Holy Spirit blessing movement for a godly America.

"IT TAKES TWO, GOD and YOU"

"KEEP LOOKING UP"

Thank my Lord Jesus Christ for both those blessing words with those wonderful Bible verses that was given me to write in order that everyone will believe the Word of God and His Son being our Salvation Savior. My Brothers and Sisters in Christ lets become more faithful believers that God will bless and heal our country. The heart-beat of this book that you and those love ones with your faith be born again or saved thru the grace and love of our Lord Jesus Christ by having that ever-lasting salvation free gift and for that heavenly home. Those born again faithful Christians thru death, your soul or spirit will go to the third Heaven and be there until the coming Rapture of His church.

The real backbone of this book for those born again faithful married couples and their children be looking up, always be ready, and always be watching when Jesus come in the air for His Church. This Rapture will become a life time Heavenly Journey all done in God's glory. With a short summary of this life time journey: After the Rapture those born again Christians with those glorious bodies will be living with our Lord Jesus Christ in the Heaven of all heaven. All faithful Christians will missed the total seven years during the Tribulation and the terrified God's wraths of the Great Tribulation. From heaven be the second coming of our Lord Jesus with the Angels and all the Saints, which are the born again faithful people. Be preparing for the great Battle of Armageddon, the War of all wars, against Satan the devil, the Antichrist the beast, and the False Profit with their army of two hundred-million, all being defeated by the Word of God. Next, we will be living in the Millennium period for one thousand years with our Lord Jesus and all the Saints. The old will passed away with the coming wonderful new heaven, the new earth, and the Holy City of the New Jerusalem. This New Jerusalem created by our Heavenly Father will be coming down from the Heaven of heaven in glory and grace. Those born again Christians will be living in this Holy City of the New Jerusalem with our Lord Jesus Christ and all the Saints for evermore.

The following Bible verse tells it all what has happen and what the future holds for our America, we must be praying for bigger faithful changes.

> If my people, who are called by my name, will humble themselves and pray and seek my face and turned from wicked ways, then will I hear from heaven and will forgive their sins and will heal their land.
> (2 Chronicles 7:14)

ONE

My God Blessings

Let's begin this chapter with a fresh start for any new year and those future happy New Years. Those people staying up late or past the mid night hour on the last night of the old year by seeing the big ball of NYC coming down for the New Year. For its party time seeing everyone having a big good old time by leaving the old year and bring in the new year. For us old timers we been there and done all that party time many years ago. Beside we are in bed by 10:30 o'clock after watching by TV, the wild western of Gun-Smoke, the musical show of Lawrence Welk, and the late news. Now for all those big dreams and those new honey cover hopes in your mind for the New Year resolutions for the world to see. What happen? Few days later all those big dreams and sweet hopes are all forgotten, well maybe next year. That is God's willing and the creak don't rise.

This is perfect time for the new year by asking our Heavenly Father for wisdom to refresh and restore our body, heart, mind, and soul. Those daily prayers for your purpose needs, our Heavenly Father and our Lord Jesus will hear and answer those special needs for yourself and for your family. Start out with that big Top of the Morning with a hot shower and one of those He-Man breakfast which will charged up your body, heart, mind and soul. Always take time with your family for those daily Bible reading and study times, togetherness for daily prayer times, going church together each week, and for those happy precious family times. Togetherness make a greater marriage relationship and wonderful family relationship. Most important of all for your own personal salvation with these words.

> Dear Lord Jesus, I know that I am a sinner, I ask forgiveness by turning from my sinful ways for you come into my heart and life.

> You died on the cross for my sinful life with your alive resurrection as my Lord and my Savior for my forever heavenly lasting salvation.

> In the name of Jesus, Amen.

At this time will share some outstanding words for this New Year by Billy Graham daughter, Anne Graham Lotz, taken from the Decision Magazine dated January 2022.

> Praise God! During this New Year, let your life like Peter's, bear witness that our God is Lord of the slim change, the fat change, the no change, and the second change. So answer His recall to discipleship now.

Tune your ears to His voice as you read His Word and ask Him to refill you.

Open your heart to be restored in love for Him and service to Him.

Then refocus your entire life on Jesus as you follow Him. He will lead you to a cross. Deny yourself and take it up. But don't forget. After the cross comes the resurrection and the power and the glory and the crown!

And maybe -just maybe -this is the year we will see Him face to face.

Just like those above words, it can be like that old song. "Face to Face with Christ."

Face to face with Christ, my Savior, Face to face-what will be,

When the rapture I be-hold Him, Jesus Christ who died for me.

Face to face I shall be-hold Him, far beyond the starry sky,

Face to face in all His glory, I shall see Him by and by.

Our Heavenly Father has a plan and purpose for all His children. So plan wisely for those big dreams and those bigger goals in your own life journey. You may be at slower start in your valley of those dreams and bigger goals, but the all mighty God will take you all the way to the very mountain top with bigger dreams of greater goals with Victory. Our Lord Jesus is always there for you and your family with all those dreams of goals. Just lay all those positive needs at His feet and leave them there by receiving positive results.

My Lord Jesus Christ had a plan and purpose for me in my ninety "Golden Years. What happen and did happen, now for rest of the story. One morning at 2:30, got up go to the bathroom with my prostate problems. Next sit down on my couch drinking some water with a short time for cat napping. I don't for sure what happen next next, received this message of a calling from my Lord Jesus to wrote a book. With my How? The answer was like a mild soft voice, maybe a whisper. "It's not your will, but my will for I am more willing provided those words with Bible verses. He lay on my heart to write for His Glory these two books: "It Takes Two, God and You" and "Keep Looking Up" for they are His books. It became a new chapter of bigger goals and wonderful purpose for my life journey. My Lord Jesus Christ gave me those wisdom words and the key Bible verses, it's like He is talking to me while I'm listening. As I am typing on my lap-top one finger at a time, those words just came to me. Have you ever read a book that it's so good, you can't put it down by wanting to read another chapter or two? That is how I feel by reading and study five chapters in my Bible each day of learning more about God's plans, promises, and purpose for my life journey. What are your future life time dream for bigger goals? Anything can happen and will happen with God's Blessings just for you.

For I have blessed your country from the very beginning of the 1600's to the present twenty-first century. For it is my wake-up calling for repentance and forgiveness the sins and terrible violence of your country for they have become like those in Noah times before the flood."

Wake-up sleeping America! Now more than ever it's time for a Holy Spiritual Revival come across our America and rest of the whole wide world. For all this to happen the church and those prayers warriors must get on their knees with those reaching-out hands toward heaven for that total repentance come into our daily lives in order save our country. With that extra calling from our Heavenly Father, lets joint togetherness for carrying that wooden Cross for our Lord Jesus that extra mile or two. By getting more people born again or saved before the coming Rapture for the Heavenly Father wants His Kingdom filled up with believers that no one be left behind. Our Heavenly Father will give us that blessing Faith, greater Hope, and wonderful Love that can last our lifetime, Amen in Jesus name.

There been several times my old lap top would mess up big time which give me fits. I took those lap top wild problems and lay them at my Savior's feet and leave them there without any fear. Having more faith and less fear when you lay those daily concerns at His feet. As always be praising your Heavenly Father for answer those life journey dreams of bigger goals when you lay them at feet, never fear.

At this time to share those wonderful words written by Billy Graham wife, Ruth Bell Graham, from Ruth's Attic which is a selection of her writings.

"At His Feet."

> Lay them quietly at His feet one by one; each
> desire, however sweet, just begun; dreams
> still hazy, growing bright; hope just poised,
> winged for flight; all your longing each delight
> every one.

> At His feet and leave them there, never fear;
> every heartache, crushing care trembling fear
> crushing care- trembling tear; you will find
> Him always true, men may fail you, friends
> be few,
> He will prove Himself to you far more dear.

IT TAKES TWO, GOD and YOU with those life time
concerns just lay them at His feet without any fear.

TWO

Blessing Marriage and Family Relationship

The next two chapters consisting how the Bible and the Church is important to you, your family, your friends, and mostly for those spiritual unsaved. For it takes God's Word with the love of Jesus of restoring your body, heart, mind, and soul by having that greater outstanding marriage and family relationship. Let's take a closer look together of the many Bible verses and the words of God creation for that faithful marriage relationship that of one man as the husband and one woman as his wife being of one flesh.

> "IT TAKES TWO, GOD and YOU"
> In the beginning God said "IT TAKE TWO."

> God said "Let us make man in our image, in our likeness." So God created man in his own image, in the image of God he created him. (Genesis 1: 26-27)

But for Adam no suitable helper was found.

So the Lord God cause the man to fall into a deep sleep; and while he was sleeping, he took one of man's ribs and closed up the place with flesh. Then the Lord God made a woman from the rib he had taken out of the man, and he brought her to the man. The man said "This is now bone of my bones and flesh of my flesh; she shall be called woman for she was taken out of man." For this reason a man will leave his father and mother and be united to his wife, and they shall become one flesh.
(Genesis 2: 20-24)

Beginning the Creator made both man and woman.
For this man will leave his father and mother and be united with his wife, and the two will become one flesh.
They are no longer two, but one. Therefore what God has joined together, let man not separate.
(Matthew 19: 4-6)

According the Bible the first marriage was created by our Heavenly Father that of man and woman, that of Adam and Eve. This is God's purpose for man will leave his father and mother, not for man be under the protective custody of his parents. For that faithful man with his faithful wife be able established a greater new family relationship. Together as husband and wife, they will be able have an inseparable union with one flesh. This is true from the very beginning of time with Adam and Eve and up to the present twenty-first century. No courts, kings, queens, or any presidents from any country or nation should Not change God's purpose with marriage. Which is between one man as the husband and one woman as his wife. Sadly, this has changed in the last few years of this twenty-first century regarding with same-sex marriage. That kind of marriage with two gay men or the marriage of two women known as lesbians. Yes, it has happened in our America by the approval by the Supreme Court with the greater approval by the unfaithful Forty-fourth President. As Paul Harvey would tell it on national radio stations few years ago; "Now for Rest of the Story."

The Supreme Court made the final approval decision for same-sex marriage rights with vote of 5 to 4 to be applied for all fifty states. This higher court of America voted what the unfaithful Forty-fourth President wanted, not according to God's Word found in the Bible. With the request of this president, the White House was lighted up in rainbow colors to celebrate the Supreme Court decision on same-sex marriage. Can you believe this absurd decision, but it happened in our own country! Various polls at that time the majority of Americans want to see the higher court of our country make the final ruling. It was a vote whether states can continue defining marriage as the union of one man and one woman, or give two gay men and that of two women known as lesbians the right to marry. Prior to that decision by the higher court that same-sex couples could marry in thirty-six states and the District of Columbia. We are now seeing this same situation regarding same-sex marriage in other countries around the world. In this case the U.S. Supreme Court and the unfaithful Forty-fourth President did not set a good Christian example for our America.

Many church pastors, ministers, and priests don't agree with the higher court decision and the absurd approval by that unfaithful president regarding the issue for same-sex marriage. These faithful men and women of God welcome those couples come to their church, but not like this kind of sin against God by performing same-sex marriage in their own church. What will the future hold for the church of America? Will the federal courts fine the church with many law suits or the government take away their tax freedom for not obeying the law performing same-sex marriage? The American faithful taxpayers could see their tax deductions for church contribution be taken away by the unfriendly IRS. Only time will tell regarding this sad situation. This is a wake-up call from God for this sinful situation and other conditions that facing our country.

The good news while in office the Forty-fifth President appointed three more conservative faithful Judges to the U.S. Supreme Court and appointed 300 faithful federal judges across our America all within four years in his first term as our faithful president. All these appointed Christian minded conservative Judges will provide good ole fashion and lasting Bible principles for our country that will last many years yet to come or when our Lord Jesus comes for the Rapture.

According to our Heavenly Father, marriage is between one man and one woman, that has always been true since the days with Adam and Eve. All children need one man as the father and one woman as the mother as caring faithful parents. During these uncertain times so many children don't have a father living at home anymore (25 percent), leaving behind a wife as a single mother for those hurting children. With both faithful parents as a father and as a mother, that their children can have a better education, emotional stability, and good ole fashion Christian morals. Faithful married parents of togetherness must read and study the Bible each day, be praying each day, and going church each week for having that happy family relationship. Faithfulness makes a powerful-stronger country that will last many generations.

IT TAKES TWO, GOD and YOU require family Bible study time, family Prayer time, family Church time, and family fun time.

The greatest thing parents can and should do for their children is sow faith seeds in the hearts and minds for their children's salvation. Provided for them good education such as a degree from good trade-vocation school, community college, or some university is now required for having well-paid jobs and good benefits in your children's career. As faithful parents let your children know more than anything else in this world, that you want them become faithful Christians. That kind of family faithfulness in turn makes a greater stronger America that can last many years yet to come. As faithful parents, you should always love your children and their children and tell them how you care and love them from your heart. Those little children are the joy and pride for their parents and grandparents from the day they were born, during those school years, into their adult life as they leave home. Always put the love of Jesus in your children's hearts, minds, and their soul which will lead into better faithful lifestyle for those little or older love ones. Our Lord Jesus always want our life at its fullness by having greater faith, more joy, much love, and that outstanding living peace.

Parents, there is a time to correct your children with a spanking or good talking with the right words that is best for your child. Parents need both understanding and wisdom with the proper loving attitude for their children before discipline them. Never say to a child or an adult "You never amount to anything" or "You are worthless, wish you were never born." Unkind words like those have harmful mental or physical conditions on any young or older person for life. There is a proper or right time to talk with your children regarding "the facts of life" that of marriage and sex. The father should talk with his sons and the mother should talk with her daughters, so your children don't hear or experience about sex the first time from other school students. Depend on the condition or situation, it may require both parents with that talking to their child or children. During good times or hard times under various conditions, your children and your grandchildren may need Christian advice regarding their financial or marriage problems. As faithful parent and grandparents take that extra time providing good helpful sound advice, if necessary or possible some helpful financial support for your love ones. Again, as good advice take that extra time and more quality time for those prayerful needs with your love ones. Teach your children and those grandchildren the Bible values of the three T's, that is with proper training, teaching, and trusting God.

> My son, do not despise the Lord's discipline
> and do not decent his rebuke, because the Lord
> disciplines those he loves, and as a father's the
> son he delight in.
> (Proverbs 3:11-12)

My son, keep your fathers' commands and do not forsake your mother's teaching. Bind them upon your heart forever; fasten them around your neck. When you walk, they will guide you; when you sleep, they will watch over you; when you awake; they will speak to you. For these commands are a lamp, this teaching is a light, and the corrections of discipline are the way of life.
(Proverbs 6: 20-23)

Discipline your son, for in that there is hope.
(Proverbs 19:18)

Our attitude should be the same as that of Christ Jesus.
(Philippians 2:5)

One of my best life experience as a father, husband, and as parent was when my wife and myself bought this property consisting both newer house and barn on four acres of land there in mid-Indiana. That spring our teenage two sons and I fenced in the pasture, then we got two half grown calves to raise. That fall we had them butcher, one for our freezer and sold the other one for someone else freezer. Yes, we got the family a quarter horse which we name Candy Bar. We join the 4-H Club with my helping hand of being accountant became their treasure, and our daughter rode the horse in western-like contest by being real proud of winning blue ribbons and trophies. We became urban cowboys and call our little big spread the Circle R Ranch. It took that old fashion family team-work as we all work together with many chores: clean out the barn, feeding time, putting up hay, time in garden plus canning those vegetables, and cutting one acre of grass. As always there was school home work to do and at last family relaxing time with games and watching TV.

We had our family togetherness with church and Sunday school, the drive-in movies, swimming at the YMCA, the county and Indiana state fairs, plus local towns activities. Always took couple weeks of vacation from my accounting work by taken our travel trailer going camping at Turkey Run State Park which is located in western Indiana. Those fifteen camping years going this Indiana State Park, our family enjoy many activities with camp fires of outdoor cooking, or eating great meals at the Turkey Run Inn, canoe trips down Sugar Creek, horse-back riding, swimming, and many walking trails. Those were good happy Hoosier years by going camping as a family of togetherness. This state park is located near Rockville, Indiana of Parke County which have more covered bridges than any America's county. Twice each year in the Spring and the Fall seasons its big fun times in Rockville with different wonderful events around the town square and a big must of seeing those old wooden cover bridges thru out Parke County. Also, near Rockville visit that ole time Billie Creek Village. Family time of togetherness are always great happy times. Years later of those retirement wonderful "Golden Years" by looking back in time will be saying with words "Yes, those were wonderful time of togetherness."

¶¶¶¶¶

Good ole family time of many happy life time experiences are like the week end newspaper comics that of the Family

Circus. What they experience as a family are alike any American family, even just like yours. It will bring back those family precious memories of those fun and good times, even like going to grandpa and grandma house for great Thanksgiving turkey dinner and having those Merry Christmas with gifts.

The days of this twenty-first century it's big must that your children have good education so they have good head start in their careers for rest of their life. Those young people that just graduated from high school or higher education at some university, first of all they need to learn about the value of hard work. Stop wishing, start doing. That is by starting from the bottom at their job and then work-up the successful step ladder by taken one step at a time for that future better goal. It's lways better going forward in your lifetime career or job than going backwards. The same advice with buying a house or renting, those young married couples should start first by renting an apartment and years later with more money saved up with bigger down payment to buy that dream home. It took your dad and mom many hard working years in their lifetime obtained all the good things as new car, furniture, and a nice home. Those parents know for sure all those nice things must be fully paid before those retirement years. In the last few years during this twenty-first century, there are those young people moving back home with their parents mainly because of financial reasons or marriage problems. In those conditions, parents should show greater kindness and be more understanding with those unknown situations by providing good sound advice to those love ones or little pep talk will be most helpful. As always keep-on praying for those love ones for this shows greater love for them. Any young married couples still facing with any financial concerns, my good advice be talking with your church pastor or with a faithful good honest money manager. Otherwise, there will be more financial and marriage problems down the road that anyone can't cope with.

> Children's children are a crown to the aged,
> and parents are the pride of their children.
> (Proverbs 17:6)
>
> Bringing up children showing hospitality.
> (1Timothy 5:10)

The Bible is the only book for teaching proper training for your children and their children the love of our Lord Jesus. Jesus said "Bring the children to me for the kingdom of heaven belonged to these children." He is the one that will take those children in his arms, put his hands on them and blessed them. In order get into that Heavenly Father kingdom, children must learn about God's love so they can love and obey him.

The following are some good Christian principles of teaching your children and their children while they are still young in heart and mind:

- Teach them the importance of God by going Church for their Salvation, study the Bible and prayer time.
- Teach them the importance of authority, finance, honesty, and loyalty.
- Teach them the importance of love, obey, respect, trust, and the value of hard work.

Honor your father and mother as the Lord commanded you that you may live long and that you may go well.
(Deuteronomy 5:16)

Love the Lord your God with all your heart and with all your soul and with all your strength. These commandments that I give you to be on your hearts. Impress them on to your children.
(Deuteronomy 6:5-7)

Children obey your parents in the Lord, for this is right.
Honor your father and mother which is the first commandment with a promise-that it may go well with you and that you may enjoy instead, bring them up in the training and instructions of the Lord.
(Ephesians 6:1-4)

Educate your children to self-control ... and you have done much to abolish misery from their future.
Daniel Webster

Marriage involves Christian commitment between husband as a believing Christian man with his wife as a believing Christian woman being faithful and royal to each other as long as they both live. This is from their or your wedding vow which is, "until death do us apart." Wedding vows are the new beginning in your marriage life by sharing the good with the bad and staying faithful and royal to each other. When it comes to commitment, just try be like our Lord Jesus as he asked His twelve disciples for total commitment. He meant it as the same level for devotion. Those disciples leave their old ways of making a living and make a new beginning by walking with Jesus all the way. Lord Jesus was saying to His disciples" are you willing to go all the way, this will not be easy." This is true today in this twenty-first century "are you willing go all the way" to carry the cross for your Lord Jesus? He was right "This will not be easy."

> Then Jesus said to his disciples, "If anyone
> come after me, he must deny himself and take
> up his cross and follow me."
> (Matthew 16:24)

Giving was always part of God's divine purpose for us, which means we already have what we need in order to begin sharing with others. The Following are some Bible verses and wise sayings for your giving to any good charity organization and to your church:

> In tithes and offerings. Bring the whole tithe
> into the storehouse, that here be enough food
> in my house. Says the Lord Almighty, and see
> I will open the floodgates of heaven and pour
> all so much blessings that will not have room
> enough for it.
> (Malachi 3:8-10)

> Whoever sows sparingly will also reap sparingly,
> and who sows generously will reap generously.

Each man should give what he decided in his heart to give, for God loves a cheerful giver. And God is able to make all grace abound to you, so that in all things at all times, having all you need, you will abound in ever abound in ever good works. As it is written:
He has scattered abroad his gifts to the poor; his righteousness endures forever.
(2nd Corinthians 9:6-9)

We make a living by what we get God has given us two hands—one to receive with and the other to give with.
Billy Graham

First, Work hard, gained you can, and Second saved all you can,
Then give all you can.
John Wesley

Are you giving to God what is right, or what is left?
Unknown

Give not from the top of your purse, but from the bottom of your heart.
Unknown

Just remember there is no perfect marriage. Always talk it over with each other to address any difference what to do with your family's financial, health issues, and other marriage problems how to solve them. Never give up, keep on believing for your God is there for anyone, anytime, and anywhere. We must set a good example in forgiveness, just look at the Bible story of Joseph in the book of Genesis. Jacob had twelve sons, Joseph was one of the youngest and the favorite. As a sign with his favoritism, Jacob gave Joseph a beautiful coat "of many colors." Because of this colorful coat and his dreams against his brothers, those ten brothers wanting get even against him, so his brothers sold Joseph into slavery to Egypt. Years later Pharaoh made Joseph ruler over Egypt, this was the results of many interpreted of dreams by Joseph for seeing the coming seven years of Egypt's great food abundance and later the coming seven years of sever famine. Joseph had the power of life and death over people and with his ten brothers when they came the first time to Egypt for food. But he chose to forgive them and feed all his brothers and his father during this time of famine. When it comes to forgiveness don't pass the buck lets buried the hatchet. For that total living peace in your heart and mind, just take away any anger against anyone before your bedtime or the coming sunset. Otherwise, without forgiveness there be everlasting bitterness against each other. This is very true for I known of two men had this anger and bitterness over some small grievance, but it became too late when one of them died first without any forgiveness. With those words of your forgiveness, God will bless you and your family with many showers of blessings with a life time "of many colors." We can be like our Lord Jesus with His love in forgiveness, just have more love in your heart with forgiveness for others.

Who is this who even forgives sins?
(Luke 7:49)

Be kind and compassionate to one another,
forgiving each other, just as Christ God
forgave you.
(Ephesians 4:32)

Bear with each other and forgive whatever
grievances you may have against another.
Forgive as the Lord forgave you. And over all
these virtues put on love, which binds them all
together in perfect unity.
(Colossians) (3:13-14)

It's always best to take those family and financial problems to the Lord in prayer for He will answer and solved any problems that are facing you or your family. Also, it's best talk with your church pastor by getting his or her viewpoints as you face those dark storms in your life or in your marriage. If you have the faith of a small mustard seed, God will take away those mountain high difficulties or problems in your life. At times your life difficulties and problems seems like the sky is falling on your marriage which in turn hurting your family. You might be saying these words "Lord, what are we going to do," or "Our marriage is going nowhere, ready to throw up my hands and give up." Never be too proud or shame to asked Him, because your Heavenly Father will answer those prayers of many needs.

There in Boys Town, Omaha, Nebraska there is large statue of bigger boy carry his smaller brother on his back. Under the statue are the words "He Ain't Heavy, Father ... He's M' Brother!" God answer all those prayers years ago for Father Flanagan with the impossible dream for building Boys

Town. In the 1940's Hollywood made a great movie about the starting-up times of Boys Town, starting Spencer Tracy as Father Flanagan and Mickey Rooney as one of the boys. This is an outstanding town for the young ones without any faithful loving family home. It's a home where no one has a past and everyone has a future. Boy Town's slogan: Saving Children 100 years Healing Families. Our country been very blessed and thankful for people like Father Flanagan. Brothers and Sisters in Christ what are your dreams making our America become greater? Maybe God is calling you do something great for Him, be like Father Flanagan and dream big by receiving that greater goal. Please join with me with your financial support for homes like Boys Town.

> The work will continue you see, whether I am there or not, because it is God's work, not mine.
> Father Flanagan

Father Flanagan had lots of heavy burdens on his back, but he took those heavy burdens to the Heavenly Father. If you and your family are having heavy burdens, you may be saying "We can't take this anymore just feel like given up." Just take those heavy burdens off your back and give them to the Son of God. Just do your best for He will do the rest. Jesus will say to you "These burdens are not heavy, you are my brothers and sisters. I will carry them for you." Having Jesus in your life, always take time to praised and thank Him what He has done for you and your family. Our Heavenly Father and His Son, our Lord Jesus Christ, are always able and more willing to carry those heavy burdens.

During these many unknown times of this dark world, it may feel there is no hope or feeling hopeless. The answer my Brothers and Sisters for that blessing Faith, greater Hope, and lasting Love is only found in the Bible, the Word of God. This is the right time to start-up a good Spiritual Program for yourself and your family consisting with daily Bible reading and study time, daily Prayer time, and Sunday Worship time. Keep on praying and let the Word of God with the Love of Jesus encourage you. Just count your blessings every day, His love for you will become the Blessing of all blessings. Our Lord Jesus will bring much joy each morning into your life as He see your face at every sunrise. For He will brighten your life with greater sunshine during the daytime and during the early evening hours, your life will become more brighter and more wonderful than the most colorful western sky sunset. Jesus will bless your life and your family with many rainbow colors with showers of blessing for those tomorrows yet to come. Just keep on the sunny side of life by keep looking up.

I will challenge you and your family to read and study the entire Bible each year. Here is an easy plan, just read and study five chapters each day. You have read the entire Bible from Genesis to Revelation, 1,189 chapters or 31,100 verses, completely through in one year. Over the years by reading and study of God's Word, I have learned more about the outstanding love of my Lord Jesus. Feel free to high-light or marks those key Bible verses that touch your heart. Let your Bible become the master peace-maker for show and tell. My first wife's Bible was so worn out of being used over the years it was taped together. She told me "No new Bible, I had this one as a little girl." Read and study the Bible each day will help you and your family build-up your confidence, make better decision, reduce stress, resist temptation, and improve your thinking. Most important of all, you can share your Bible and your faith with others. Jesus said "Heaven and earth will pass away, but my word will never pass away."

You might be saying this is ole fashion for these times of the twenty-first century, but it is a good new fashion by reading and study the Bible each day. The final results of reading and study each day, you be loving your Lord Jesus with all your heart and with all your soul. Your marriage partnership and your family partnership of loving each other, will become just as our Lord Jesus loved His Church. Come grow old with total togetherness for that everlasting love in your marriage, that you belong as one flesh for a lifetime with that true love for each other. This is God's plan and purpose for that everlasting loving marriage relationship and later for that everlasting parent relationship. With these two everlasting relationships, you and your family will become heavenly minded with Bible verses.

> Each man should have his own wife, each wife her own husband.
> The husband should fulfill his marital duties to his wife, and likewise the wife to her husband.
> The wife's body does not belong to her along but also to her husband. In the same way, the husband's body does not belong to him along but also to his wife.
> (1 Corinthians 7:2-4)

A woman is bound to her husband as long he lives.
But if the husband dies, she is free to marry anyone she wishes, but he must belong to the Lord.
(1 Corinthians 7:39)

Wives, submit to your husband as to the Lord. For the husband is the head of the wife as Christ is the head of the Church, his body, of which he is the Savior. Now as the church submits to Christ, so also wives should submit to their husbands in everything. Husbands, love your wife, just as Christ loved the church and gave himself up for her to make her holy, cleansing her by the washing with water through the word, and to present her to himself as a radiant church, without stain or wrinkle or any other blemish, but holy and blameless. In the same way, husbands ought to love their wives as their own bodies. He who loves his wives loves himself.
After all, no one ever hates his own body, but he feeds and care for it, just as Christ does the church—for we are members of his body.
For this reasons a man will leave his father and mother and be united to his wife, and the two will become one flesh. This is a profound mystery-but I am talking about Christ and the church.

However, each one of you also must love his wife as he loves himself, and the wives must respect her husband.
(Ephesians 5: 22-33)

That true statement "They say that the job of a housewife is never done." Every day should be Mother Day, do you understand that husbands and tell that to your children. Make each day Thanks-giving and at the same time Thanks-living for your love ones. All fathers and mothers as faithful parents should be working together with love by raising your young or older children, your job for sure is never done. Don't let the job become too big for yourself, just do your part and your Lord Jesus will do more of his part. We must be praying for our children and their children all the time, even from the years as caring babies, during those school years, and those young adults moving out of their parent's home for the first time for higher education or marriage. Following some wisdom words for mothers by Ruth Bell Graham, the wife of Billy Graham, it really sums it all up for Mother Day or any day for mothers:

We mother must take care of the impossible and trust God for the impossible. We are to love, affirm, encourage, teach, listen, and care for the physical needs of the family. I have as a wife and mother a good cause—the best cause in the world, but I lack the shoulders to support it. The job isn't too big for me. I am not big enough for the job. As a mother, I must faithfully, patiently, lovingly, and happy do my part—then quickly wait for God to do his.

> In the same way, let your light shine before
> men, that they see your good deeds and praise
> your Father in heaven.
> (Matthew 5:16)

All those daughters and daughter-in-law will someday become future mothers, will leave you some words of wisdom.

> Embrace your life's journey by looking forward
> what is important for your future marriage by
> seeking the love of Jesus with your heart and
> for God's guidance with that new husband
> by having a faithful and happy marriage
> relationship and later the family to be.
> That your Heavenly Father will provide with
> many blessings.
> Each day make Lord Jesus become bigger part
> in your life, your family, and your friends, this
> will become the blessing for everybody.

This world during this new twenty-first century is full of many unknowns. Your own answer to your own problems maybe just blowing in the wind. It's prayer time so get on your knees, our God in heaven will hears those prayers and He answer those prayers for He has a plan and purpose just only for you. Nothing is too small or too big for our God by solving those trouble concerns facing you each day. Just take that extra time each day to read and study your Bible for the real answers for there is a special verse just for your own situation. For sure those wonderful blessings came from our Heavenly Father that something good will happen in your life. It will become seeing by believing with your faithfulness in your Heavenly Father and the tender loving for you from your Lord Jesus.

It's like the story in your Bible of King Solomon. God came to King Solomon in a dream and said to him. "Ask Me whatever you wish, and I will give it to you." King Solomon did not ask for riches, but he ask for "Understanding heart be able govern the people of Israel." God bless him with that loving heart with greater knowledge and that outstanding leadership of wisdom. He became the wealthy person during his life time and the wisest man ever lived. Yes, it can happen to you just asked him for He will say "Ask Me whatever you wish, and I will give it to you." Pray in Jesus name for those unreal needs and He will give you back positive realistic results.

> Instruct a wise man and he will be wiser still;
> teach a righteous man and he will add to is
> learning.
> (Proverbs 9:9)

> A man of understanding delights in wisdom.
> (Proverbs 10:23)

> We know also that the Son of God has come
> and given us understanding, so that we may
> know him who is true. And we are in him who
> is true, even in his Son Jesus Christ. He is the
> true God and eternal life.
> (1 John 5: 20)

> I never learn anything from talking, I only
> learn things when I ask questions.

The Fighting Irish of Notre Dame University
Football Coach Lou Holtz

Some wise words from President Abraham Lincoln "It is not the years in your life that counts, but the life in your years." While you were in your mother's womb, God has great plans and purpose for each person. Let Him cleanse and shape you into the person you were created to be. Let God with the Holy Spirit speak to you about your life and His plans and that bigger purpose for you. Just forget the past years let's start with the present and start living for the future. When the Holy Spirt is directing and living within us, God will shape each person becoming faithful fishers of men for his Son, our Lord Jesus Christ. My dear Brothers and Sisters be sure that you use those gifted talents for the glory of God. You are never too young or too old to start using those God's gifted talents. Become like the good Shepherd for he will guides you in paths of righteousness. Let's become more the concerns for others by telling the Heavenly Father "Here I am ready to carry the Salvation Cross for the world Savior, Lord Jesus Christ."

> In the same way, let your light shine before
> men, that they may see your good deeds and
> praise your Father in heaven.
> (Matthew 5:16)

I would like for you be free from concern.
unmarried man is concerned about the Lord's
affairs—how he can please the Lord.
But a married man is concerned about the
concerned about the affairs of this world—
how he can please his wife—and his interest

are divided. An unmarried woman or virgin is concerned about the Lord's affairs. Her aim is to be devoted to the Lord in both body and spirit. But a married woman is concerned about the affairs of this world—how she can please her husband. I am saying this for your good, not to restrict you, but may live in a right way in undivided devotion to the Lord. (1Corinthians 7:32-35)

Just remember that our Heavenly Father is more willing to help anyone, any time of the day or night or anywhere you might be. He is always there to take care of your family concerns, your broken down finances, your health conditions, your marriage problems, and any other many needs. He will use you for His glory at the same time He is always able holding you in His big strong arms. According to the words in the Bible, God is the head of Christ, Christ is the head of the Church, and the husband is the head for his wife. Christ submitted to God, faithful husbands submitted to Christ, and those believing faithful wives submitted to their faithful godly husbands.

Wives, in the same way be submissive to your husbands. Husbands, in the same way be considerate as you live with wives, and treat them with respect as the weaker partner. (1 Peter 3:1,7)

IT TAKES TWO, GOD and YOU by having the Love of Christ.

THREE

Bible Love Stories

There will be lots of those little sweet or unsweat talks in your marriage years, just remember tell your husband, your wife, your children, your grandchildren, and rest your family and friends those sweet three words; "I love you" or "We love you." Those nice sweet words must come from your heart. What a big difference that will make in those people lives, for they will know for sure that someone cares and love them. Just as God loves us, we must love others with lots of care and kindness. As faithful parents, you are always there with your love for your children from the time your new born baby, those children growing up years, and when your children start having your grandchildren. God calls us to live a life with that forever faith, greater joy, more love, and much lasting peace in our body, heart, mind, and soul. God with His Son, our Lord Jesus, are the only blessing hope and greater lasting love for you and your family. Yes, it takes faith, hope, and love for that greater happy marriage. As parents and new grandparents always keep in mind with the following suggestion: being caring, humble, loving, and patience. Always walk by faith not by sight for Jesus uses the seen to point out the unseen. Our Lord Jesus will turn your marriage around and let it become the Heavenly Sunlight, which will become the everlasting brighter sunshine in the lives of your love ones. Let your light be shinning just as Jesus is the lighthouse into the darkness of the whole wide world.

> For with you is the foundation of life; in your
> light we see light.
> (Psalm 36:9)
>
> My God is the light of life.
> (Psalm 56:13)
>
> Blessed are those who have learned to acclaim
> you, who walks in the light of your presence,
> O Lord.
> (Psalm 89: 15)
>
> You are light in the Lord. Live as children
> of light (for the fruit of light consists in all
> goodness, rightness, and truth) and find out
> what pleases the Lord.
> (Ephesians 5:8)

At times during our life journey by using that good ole fashion common sense, just like the faithful older Amish people with their wisdom or it's like the old Amish saying in Lancaster County, Pennsylvania some years ago:

"Let things be, not being control of everything or everyone."

Give me happiness, O Lord, for I give myself to you.
O Lord, you are so good, so ready to forgive, so full of unfailing love for all who ask for your help.
(Psalm 86: 4-5)

You are my refuge and my shield; I have put my hope in you.
(Psalm 119:114)

The Lord will keep you from harm-he will watch over your life; the Lord will watch over your comings or going both now and forevermore.
(Psalm 121:7-8)

But let him ask in faith, with no doubling, for he doubts is like a wave of the sea driven and tossed by the wind.
(James 1:6)

Humble yourself, therefore, under God's mighty hand, that he may lift you up in due time. Cast all your anxiety on him because he cares about you.
(1 Peter 5 7)

How about going back maybe 250 years ago with more of that ole fashion common senses from those written words by Benjamin Franklin of his book, Poor Richard Almanac: Sleeping fox catches no poultry, one day is worth two tomorrows, diligence is the mother of good luck, early to bed and early to rise provides a man with security, money reward, and opportunity for personal advancement, lastly penny save is penny earned.

Man must pick the right soul mate for his wife and woman must pick the right soul mate for her husband. Being faithful Christian is a must for yourself and your mate, this give you both a better faithful head start for that blessing, greater, and long lasting marriage relationship. Our Heavenly Father with His many blessings will provide those greater plans and purpose for your marriage, your family or a future family. All it takes from the husband and his wife by having that greater lasting marriage and family relationship is more of your faith and many prayers. Like the story regarding Ruth Bell Graham, the wife of Billy Graham, in her marriage dreams she select the right man for marriage. Not the others she might date before she met the Preacher for God, who later became the America's Pastor.

I will be sharing with you four of the very best love stories found in the Bible, hoping you agree with my opinion?

In the Bible there is this outstanding story finding the right person for marriage that turn into true love story. Abraham was now old and well advanced in age for he did not want his son, Isaac, married daughter of the Canaanites. Abraham by faith sent his chief steward, Eliezer to the land where Abraham came from to find a faithful wife for his son, Isaac. This servant made a long journey to a land he didn't know, the people he hadn't met, and a long trip based upon faith. He arrived with camels, the jewelry, and the dowry money. After arriving in Abraham's hometown, Eliezer prayed that the woman who offered to water his camels would be the one for his master son. This believing prayer was answer, there came this beautiful young woman to the spring with water jars. She was one of Abraham's relative, her name was Rebekah. She gave this servant water to drink plus water for his camels. With the blessings for marriage from her family, she went back with this servant for her future marriage to Isaac. It must been love at first sight for both of them as Isaac married Rebekah, she become his faithful wife for he loved her dearly. They had twin sons, their names were Esau and Jacob.

How strong is Love, it reminded me the great Bible love story about Jacob, the son of Isaac, who worked total of fourteen years for his future father-in-law. Jacob had high hopes and wishes to married Laban's younger daughter Rachel. Jacob was in love with Rachel and she was beautiful and lovely in form. After the first seven years of hard work, Laban tricked Jacob by given Jacob his older daughter, Leah, in marriage. The marriage custom during those times that the oldest daughter be the first daughter in her father's family to get married. Maybe Jacob was not aware of this marriage custom or forgotten about it, so Jacob work another seven more years in order to have the woman he wanted to married. Those total fourteen years seem like only a few months in total to Jacob because of his love for Rachel and their love for each other. This has to be real true love do you agree? The above two love story are founded in the book of Genesis of your Bible.

There is another love story in the Bible that of Boaz and Ruth, found in the book of Ruth. It's a story about Naomi and her daughter-in-law, name Ruth, they were both widows for their husbands were deceased. Naomi was returning to her hometown of Bethlehem and Ruth want to go with her mother-in-law. Ruth got job working to glean the grain fields behind the harvesters. As it turned out, she found out later that those fields belonging to Boaz for he was related to Naomi. When the landowner, Boaz, went out to survey his fields each day, he shouted to his workers "The' Lord be with you!" His workers shouted back, "The Lord bless you!" One day in this grain field Boaz asked the harvesters foreman who was that new woman working so steadily in his fields and was told she Naomi's daughter-in- law. There in those grain field they met for the first time as Boaz asked her don't go away to stay in that field and be with his servant girls to follow the harvesters. Ruth was very gentle, humble, and lovely young widow for she cared and love her mother-in-law. One night Naomi told Ruth wash, perfume yourself, and put on your best dress and go to the threshing floor where Boaz will be. At the threshing floor as she uncovered his feet and lay down with him to keep him warm. The next morning as he realized what she had done by keeping him warm during the night, he said "The Lord bless you for your kindness." This must be the very start of their loving for each other and for their future marriage. Boaz and Ruth had a son name Obed, who became the grandfather of King David and the ancestor our Lord Jesus Christ. Even today during this new twenty-first century for your own love story as it was hundreds years ago in the days Boaz and Ruth love story. The Lord will be with you and the Lord will bless you in your married years.

My dear housewives and mothers across our nation, be sure to pray in Jesus name for faith, hope, and love for your husband, your family, and those other love ones. This is also true for those hard working husbands and all the faithful fathers regarding your wife and love ones. Just take a good look in your Bible for the word of Love, there must be hundreds Bible verses related that forever lasting Love. With that deeper feeling reason for that wonderful forever lasting Love, it came from our forever loving Heavenly Father which was passed on to His Son, that Jesus loves everyone so that everyone will have that forever lasting love for others.

The greatest love story ever told or ever written is about Joseph and Mary some two thousand years ago. God send the angel Gabriel to Nazareth, a town in Galilee, to a young virgin, name Mary. She was pledge to be married to Joseph, a descendant of David. Gabriel the angel said to Mary "Greetings, the Lord is with you and you found favor with God for you will give birth to a son." Being a godly man, Joseph want a faithful wife to love for a lifetime and who share his desires to obey and honor the Lord. Mary was exactly that kind of a woman. Learning that she was pregnant before their marriage, he had thoughts privately ending their relationship in order to avoid any public shame to Mary and her family. Angel of the Lord appeared to him in a dream and said these words "Joseph, son of David, do not be afraid take Mary as your wife." The Lord turned Joseph's mourning into a great purpose. Mary who was conceived by the Holy Spirit and her baby would become the Savior of the world and his name would be, Jesus. He was the Son of God and His purpose on earth become the Salvation Savior of the whole wide world by providing healing, loving all people, preaching or teaching to anyone, and mostly providing salvation for anyone or everyone so desire. With His love for us that we will received the most precious free gift ever, that being our salvation. This greatest evangelist of all times was a true soul winner. This turn into the greatest love story of all times for God bless Joseph and Mary with their earthly son and having Jesus as the Son of God.

> I love you, O Lord, my strength.
> (Psalm 18:1)

> Surely goodness and love will follow me all the
> days of my life.
> (Psalm 23: 6)

> May your unfailing love rest upon us, O Lord
> even as we put our hopes in you.
> (Psalm 33:22)

> He who pursues righteousness and love finds
> life, prosperity and honor.
> (Proverbs 21:21)

> Let us love another, for love comes from God.
> Everyone who loves has been born of God and
> knows God.
> (1 John 4: 7)

> The best and most beautiful things in this
> world cannot be seen or even touch, they must
> felt with the heart.
> Helen Keller

Only our Heavenly Father and our Lord Jesus Christ there in heaven has the living power for our living hope and love. Just ask in Jesus's name, He will give you and your family the following: faith, health, hope, knowledge, love, salvation, wealth, and wisdom. Jesus Christ has given us the privilege of praying in His name according to His power and authority. The Bible states that Jesus's name is above every name for that greater power and authority came from His Heavenly Father. His name is always above any condition that is facing your life such as: emotional struggles, family or personal problems, financial hard times, health problems, marriage relationship concerns, and many other needs. Jesus stated "All power is given unto me in heaven and earth." In His mighty name, He will give us greater faith, more joy, and much of that everlasting outstanding love.

Don't be afraid to asked for any family or personal concerns that you may need anytime or anywhere you are now living or located. Our Lord Jesus is always with us because of His love for you and your family so you can pass that love on to others. Always be strong and feel free take that needed closer walk each day with your Savior and be talking together of being satisfied with your own life concerns. It will be just like the old gospel song:

"Just a Closer Walk with Thee"

> I am weak but Thou art strong; Jesus, keep me
> from all wrong.
> I'll be satisfied as long as I walk, let me walk
> close to Thee.
> Give thanks to the Lord, for he is good, and
> his love endures forever.
> (1 Chronicles 16:34)

Because of the Lord's great love, we are not consumed, for his compassion never fail.
They are new every morning; great is your faithfulness.
(Lamentation 3: 22-23)

You ask for, it will be done for you by my Father in heaven.
(Matthew 18:19)

Love the Lord your God with all your heart and with all your soul and with all your mind and with all your strength. Love your neighbor as yourself.
(Mark 12:31-32)

My command is this, "Love each other as I love you.
(John 14:12)

I tell you the truth, my Father will give you whatever you ask in my name.
Ask and you will receive, and your joy will be complete.
(John 16:23-24)

Dear friends, let us love one other, for love comes from God.
Everyone who loves has been born of God and knows God.
Whoever does not love does not know God, because God is love.

DON W. ROBERTSON

This is how God showed his love among us:
He sent his one and only Son into the world
that we might live through him.
This is love: not that we love God, but that
he loved us and sent his Son as an atoning
sacrifice for our sins. Dear friends, since God
loves us, we also ought to love one another,
God lives in us and his love is made complete
in us.
(1John 4:7-12)

Husband love and treat your wife as if she is the Rose of Sharon or the Lilly in the Valley. Set aside each month that caring loving time for togetherness. It can be simple as community event, good movie, picnic in the park, pizza or nice restaurant, and a nice week end or a vacation at some state or national park. Being together shows that you love each other for it's another way of caring for each other in true love. Saying nice sweat words "I can't stop loving you." You never want your husband or your wife feel unloved for this could cause disappointment, feeling being lonely, and stressed out. Later this could turn into separation and divorce. Don't let those problems of marriage get out of hand, see your church pastor or reliable marriage adviser for good advice or opinion to improve your marriage for that longer loving relationship. Because God hates divorces for it causes so many bad and hurt feelings even more when there are children still at home. Let your marriage circle be unbroken. It may become financial expensive supporting your ex-wife and for child support which can last several years. There has been situation that those same couples come to agreement and remarried again. If there is another marriage involved to another person, sometimes that second marriage is not successful. With final results be saying sweet words "Let us love each other forever as Jesus loves us." Take time to read the Bible of "Solomon's Song of Songs," the book of Love.

> He has taken me to the banquet hall and his
> banner over me is love.
> (Song of Songs 2:4)

There is this love song that came out few years ago, I purchase that tape at a local Christian book store for my second wife. So we can share it together in our remaining golden years. The name that love song "Come grow old with me." It will become the love song that will bless your hearts for many years to come. It's a must to purchase this love song even you are a young couple that is dating for future marriage or as young and older couples to improve their marriage. Saying and singing from your heart those sweet words "I and you together forever." Let your love for each other be like that our Lord Jesus, for His love is everlasting and true. Come my Brothers and Sisters in Christ let us grow old together with our Lord Jesus for that everlasting true love.

"Come grow old wit me"

> Come grow old with me.
> God bless our love
> God bless our love.

Build your family, your home, and your life on solid ground, just like the Bible story about the wise and foolish builder. That way your house and your life for your family will be built on solid rock with good cornerstones and a solid foundation. Otherwise, you and your family be standing in sinking quick sand. You can cry out to the Lord for He will hear your prayers with outstanding promises. Our Lord Jesus is the solid Rock of all Ages with tears ever flowing from heaven above just for you and your family. He is the only solid rock of your life and for the whole wide world. Let's take a closer look together from the Heavenly Father of some related Bible verses and the words about the foolish builder. It will become like that ole gospel song written by R. Kelso Carter:

"Standing on the Promises."

Standing on the promises of Christ my King.
Standing on the promises of God.
Standing on the promises of God, my Savior.

The Lord himself goes before you and will be
with you, he will never leave you nor forsake
you. Do not be afraid, do not be discourage.
(Deuteronomy 31:6)

O Lord, my Rock and my Redeemer.
(Psalm 19:14)

He along is my rock and my salvation;
he is my fortress, I will not be shaken.
He is my mighty rock, my refuge.
(Psalm 62: 6-7)

Be like the wise man who build built his house on the rock. The rain came down, the streams rose, and the winds blew and beat against the house, yet it did not fall, because it had its foundation on the rock. The foolish man built his house on sand. The rain came down, the streams rose, and the wind blew and beat against the house, and it fell with a great crash. (Matthew 7: 24-27)

My dear Brothers and Sisters in Christ, always be caring, humble, and kind to each other, and do it mostly with love. A humble thing or word with kindness and love always mean something to someone. Just be like our Lord Jesus there in your Bible, the book of John. It was before the Passover Feast that Jesus know that it was his time for him leave this world and return back to His Heavenly Father. The Father had put all things under his power, that Jesus came from heaven and returning back to his heavenly home and be with the Father. The true love story from the Son of Man loving his disciples who had followed him and carry His cross for some three years. He took off his outer clothing and wrapped a towel around his waist. He washed His twelve disciple's dirty feet and dry their feet with the towel. This was special kindness of humble love, He did this for them with that special caring of kindness and love from the Lord Jesus Christ to those He loved most.

It was just before the Passover Feast, Jesus love them with the full extent of his love. He got up from his meal, took off his outer clothing, and wrapped a towel around his waist.

After that, he poured water into a basin and
began to wash his disciples' feet, drying them
with the towel that was wrapped around him.
(John 13:1, 4-5)

Whatever your needs are, your God there in Heaven is
for anyone, anytime, and anywhere. All you need to do is
pray in Jesus name. This is a blessing and promise from our
Heavenly Father for whatever your current or those urgent
needs. Just ask in Jesus name and receive those wonderful
many blessings. There is big difference in your daily needs
and your big dream wants. Your needs are for yourself and
your family, those wants are of the world for those greedy
or selfish requests. It doesn't matter if your request is small
or big for your Heavenly Father always there for you, your
family, and your friends. Don't worry about anything, just
pray for everything of positive needs for your family and
friends. Those positive answer prayers can be for your broken
finances, health concerns, marriage relationship, and most
important that of your own or others salvation. At times
with our ocean deep worries, we feel discourage and having
feelings of just wanting just give up. Those positive prayers
be going to heaven for our Lord Jesus Christ to encourage
you and give you feelings of that living peace. God is not a
respecter of persons, what He has done for others, He can
do for you and your family. It is a true fact, that almost 90
per cent of the things we worry about don't ever happen. Just
slow-down in your busy fast life style world and just live one
day at a time for your sweet Jesus. Just put all your future
hopes in the hands of our Lord Jesus for He will guide you to
greater hopes. Christ did not offer hope only to some people

but hope to all people, mostly those unsaved ones that are not yet born again or being saved. It will become the "blessed hope" in your life for many future years yet to come. Let your prayers provide patience of hope for those many peaceful and pleasant days and times with more promise of prosperous at its fullness, always be praising the Lord Jesus.

> Put your hope in God; for I will yet praise
> Him, my Savior and God
> (Psalm 42: 5)

> May the God of hope fill you all joy and peace
> as you trust in him, so that you may overflow
> with hope by the power of the Holy Spirit.
> (Roman 15; 13)

The following are some good words of faith and wisdom from Dwight D. Eisenhower. During World War 11 in Europe, he was U.S. Army General to his fighting solders better known as Ike. Later he became a great American President. He stated these words with courage, faith, and wisdom:

"There are no atheists in foxholes."

If you are facing some foxhole situation or going through some dark storms in your lives, take time to pray in Jesus name and God will answer those prayers of many needs. God will get you out of those darker deeper foxholes of life and give you that sunny side of life. If you and your family are in a dark storm of life, God will provide peace and safety just like our Lord Jesus did when He calm that storm while those disciples were in that boat. Even when there are times of no were to turn in your life, or regarding family concerns. The question you may asked your Lord "What will we do now." My Brothers and Sisters with your answer is your own will, without the will of God those man made problems maybe blowing in the wind. My dear love ones the only answer to your daily needs is always using his authority and power to pray in Jesus name for He is always there for anyone, anytime and anywhere. You and the Son of God just take a long walk together in the coolness of some morning regarding those daily needs for yourself and family. You will be coming back praising the Son of Man with a fresh deeper warmer "coming back alive feelings." With those answer prayers for yourself and your family as you are praising the Lord Jesus, your life will become like a fully charged lifetime Die-hard Battery. He will provide for you that living Peace of God and that Peace with God for He is the total living peace for the whole wide world. There living power in prayers because there living power of the name of Jesus. Just believe and trust in your Lord Jesus with a loud "Praise the Lord" as He answer those prayers of many needs. Let's rejoiced by singing together that great joyful song written by Fanny J. Crosby:

"Praise Him! Praise Him!"

> Praise Him! praise Him! Jesus, our blessed Redeemer!
> Sing, O Earth, His wonderful love pro-claim!
> Hail Him! hail Him!
> Praise Him! praise Him! Tell of his excellent greatness,
> Praise Him! Praise Him! with joyful song.

Sing praises to God, sing praises; sing praises
to our King, sing praises.
For God is the King of all the earth; sign to
him a psalm of praise.
(Psalm 47: 6-7)

May the peoples praise you, O God; may all
the peoples praise you.
May all the nations be glad and sing for joy.
(Psalm 67: 3-4)

Trust in the Lord with all your heart, and lean
not on your own, understanding, in all your
ways acknowledge Him, and He make your
paths straight.
(Proverbs 3:5-6)

Rejoice in the Lord always. Again I say again:
Rejoice!
(Philippians 4:4)

Now faith is being sure of what we hope for
and certain of what we do not see.
(Hebrews11:1)

Teach us, O Lord, the disciplines of patience,
for to wait is often harder than work.
Peter Marshall

Our Lord Jesus will renew your strength and you will
be able to soar on the wings of the eagles. There are two
important days in our life, the day we were first born and

the day we were born again. First being born to our earthly father and mother and the day being born again as a child of our Heavenly Father. Thru the love of our Savior, we have the best free gift ever which is our own salvation. With this new salvation in our life the Heavenly Father will provide for us with greater faith, more blessing hope, newer love, and that extra strength in order that we can face those many stressful unknown days in our life journey. Because of our salvation we will be there in the Heaven of all heavens with God the Father, our Lord Jesus Christ, the Angels, and all the Saints.

> But those who hope in the Lord will renew their strength.
> They will soar on wings like eagles.
> (Isaiah 40:31)
>
> How often I have longed to gather your children together, as a hen gathers her chick under her wings.
> (Luke 14:34)

IT TAKES TWO, GOD and YOU, just only believe for our GOD is always able!

Our God in heaven is always there for anyone, anytime and anywhere. There is power in prayer, just like there is power in our Lord of hearing and answering those prayers. It like the story in the Bible the book of Daniel how Angel of God was there for Shadrach, Meshach, and Abednego in that fiery hot furnace. He always there for His children in times of temptations, trails, and troubles for He is God of that Living Love. The answer with those many life-time concerns just sow more faith seeds in your life, your forever living God will provide those greater hope with best of that living love.

It will be like priming the back yard pump that farm people had years ago, just add little water in the pump by getting back more clear cool living water from God. Your drinking cup be running over with that cool living water and you will never thirst again. His love for you with that Living Word from the Bible will become your daily bread of life as you drinking that clear cool Living Water never be thirsty again. Your well for that Living Water will never run dry, it will become the water of life. It will be like the story as Jesus talk with the Samaritan woman at Jacob's well.

> ¶ When a Samaritan came to draw water at Jacob's well Jesus was there and asked her for a drink of water.
> He told her these words "If anyone drinks this water will be thirsty again, but whoever drink the water I give him will never thirst. Indeed, the water I give him will become in him a spring of water welling up to eternal like.
> (John 4: 7, 13-14)

> To him who is thirsty I will give a drink without cost from the spring of the water of life.
> (Revelation 21: 6)

> Whoever is thirsty let him come; and whoever wishes, let him take the free gift of the water of life.
> (Revelation 22; 17)

When life seems to be unfair, God is always there to make it greater. Always have greater purpose prayer for yourself and your family, you will receive back from God much greater positive purpose during your life journey. While negative prayers are more like complaining wanting those greedy things of the world. Just believe always with greater faith through the word of God for those positive purpose prayers, our God in heaven by hearing will answer those prayers with positive purpose results. Take time each day with your family for reading and study your Bible for God's Word and thru the love of His Son, they are there for you with all the answers of your daily problems.

> For your Father knows what you need before
> you ask him.
> (Matthew 6: 8)

> Faith comes from hearing the message, and the
> message is heard through the word of Christ.
> (Romans 10:17)

When you having those worst feelings and worries regarding what will be happening today, always be hoping and praying for those better tomorrows yet to come. We never walk along as our Lord Jesus walks with us each day holding hands for we know for sure that we are in good hands with that closer walk in the light of any day. We must have those closer walk in obedience love with the Son of Man in order to obey his commands. Hoping and praying during those darken and depressing days, let God light-up those promise on your problems each day.

And this is love; that we walk in obedience to
his commands.
As you have heard from the beginning, his
command is that you walk in love.
(2 John 6)

Our Heavenly Father and our Lord Jesus as our helper
and deliver are there always with caring love for the needy,
the poor, the orphans, and the widows; He will ask "How can
I help you?" It be just like the Bible story of the poor widow
and her sons with their personal needs as God took care of
the widow's financial debt and saved her sons from slavery.

You rescue the poor from those too strong
for them, the poor and needy from them who
them.
(Psalm 35: 10)

Yet I am poor and needy; may the Lord think
of me.
You are my help and my deliverer;
O my God, do not delay.
(Psalm 40: 17)

The wife of a man from the company of the
prophets cried out to Elisha,
"Your servant my husband is dead,"
Elisha replied to her, "How can I help you?
Tell me, what do you have in your house?"
"Your servant has nothing at all," she said,
"except little oil." Elisha said, "Go, around and
ask all neighbors for empty jars.

Don't ask for just a few. Then go inside and
shut the door behind you and your sons.
Pour oil into all the jars, and as each is filled,
put it one side." They bought the jars to her and
she kept pouring. When all the jars were full,
she said to her son "Bring me another one."
Then he replied, "There is not a jar left."
Then the oil stopped flowing. She went and
told the man of God, and he said,
"Go, sell the oil and pay your debts.
You and your sons can live on what is left."
(2 King 4: 1-7)

But you know him, for he lives with you and
will be with you.
I will leave you as orphans.
(John 14: 17-18)

Religion that God our Father accepts as pure
and faultless is this: to look after orphans and
widows in their distress and to keep one from
being polluted by the world.
(James 1: 27)

You have heard that old saying that dogs are "man's best
friend. They are there for you anytime, to love you and your
family, to protected you, and always glad to see you. When
you are good to your dog, that dog always good to you. One
of my best friend was my dog, Sunshine, a sable color Sheltie
for she was with me all the time to give me her love. She
was name after that ole song of 1939 "You are my Sunshine,
don't take my Sunshine away, you are my only Sunshine."

However, there is greater friend that is our Lord Jesus Christ for He is our special Savior and our Shepherd. He is there for you anytime, to love you and your family, to protected you, and always glad to see you. Oh, what a precious friend we have in Jesus. Just like that old Gospel song.

"What a Friend We Have in Jesus."

> What a Friend we have in Jesus, all our sins
> and griefs to bear!
> What a privilege to carry Everything to God
> in prayer.

At times a family member or a close friend who are very sick with cancer, heart condition, and being sick all the time. They are just tired of living and wanting to give up. When some people wear out, they just give up. Just when that situation looks impossible, Jesus will make it possible. We will cry out to Jesus and when we do, there is a miracle or something wonderful going happen to that person. Jesus as our Healing Lord will tell us to "Rise Up for You Now Heal." There are times when doctors in hospitals can't explain for that quick recovery from those major health problem or that serious injury. Our Lord Jesus was always filled with compassion to heal the sick. The powerful name of Jesus stands for healings, miracles, and salvation. Most believing Christians know for sure that Jesus is a Miracle Son of God with His mighty healing power. Throughout the Bible, people were healed when our Lord Jesus touch them of those physical and spiritual needs. There are many Bible stories of Jesus healing with the spoken word or by his touching healing hands.

These are just few healing stories regarding people being touching by Jesus. The following healing story of this sick woman had the faith by getting on her knees and craw to Jesus in order to touch the edge of his cloak for His healing power. What great faith she had. There is another healing story taken place near the Sea of Galilee as the sick people just touched the edge of his cloak for complete healing.

A woman in a crowd who had been subject to bleeding for twelve years came up behind him and touched the edge of his cloak, she said to herself
"If I only touch his cloak, I will be healed."
Jesus turned and saw her.
"Take heart, daughter, your faith has healed you.
(Matthew 9:20-21)

People brought all the sick to him and begged him to let the sick just touched the edge of his cloak, all who touched him were healed.
(Matthew 14: 35-36)

God heals, the doctor collected the fees.
Poor Richard Almanac by Benjamin Franklin

There is Jesus healing power how He heal two blind men and heal ten men had leprosy.

Two blind followed him, calling out, "Have mercy on us, Son of David!"
When he had gone indoors, the blind men came to him, and he asked them,

IT TAKES TWO, GOD AND YOU   **55**

"Do you believe that I am able to do this?" Yes, Lord, they replied.
Then he touched their eyes and said"
According to your faith will be done to you;"
and their sight was restored.
(Matthew 9:27-30)

Now on his way to Jerusalem into a village, ten men who had leprosy met him. They stood a distance and call out a loud voice "Jesus, Master have pity on us!" When he saw them, he said "Go, show yourselves to the priests. And they went, they were cleaned.
(Luke 17:11-14)

The healing power from our Lord Jesus is a special gift of kindness and mercy. It's like the healing at the Bethesda pool. It was at the Pool of Bethesda where the sick in Jesus time gathered for healing when an angel stirred the waters. Let's take look together this healing miracle by Jesus for this hopeless paralyzed man.

Now there in Jerusalem near the Sheep Gate there is a pool. Here a great number of disable people used to lie—the blind, the lame, the paralyzed.
One who was there had been an invalid for thirty- eight years. When Jesus saw him lying there and learned that he been in this condition for a long time he asked him "Do you want to get well?"

"Sir," the invalid replied "I have no one to help me into the pool when the water is stirred. While I am trying to get in, someone else goes down ahead of me." Then Jesus said to him "Get up! Pick up your mat and walk." once the man was cured; he picked up his mat and walked. (John 5: 1-9)

There is another Bible story of healing, let me share it with you. Peter and John, disciples of Jesus went to the temple in Jerusalem to pray. They passed through the Beautiful Gate, they saw a man who had been cripple from birth. A miracle took place as Peter told the man these words: "In the name of Jesus Christ of Nazareth, rise up and walk." Another miracle of healing took place that day of the crippled beggar.

One day as Peter and John were going up to the temple at time of prayer.
Now a man crippled from birth was being carried to the temple gate called
Beautiful, where he was put very day to beg.
When he saw Peter and John, he asked them for money. Then Peter said "Look at us, no gold or silver!"
"What I do have will give you In the name of Jesus Christ of Nazareth, rise up and walk," Taking him by the right hand, he helped him up, and instantly the man's his feet and ankles became strong. He jumped up and began to walk.
(Acts 3: 1-7)

Jesus is the same healer for all people, the same healer yesterday, today, and all the tomorrows yet to come. Just believe and receive.

At times our health problems seem impossible without faith or without prayers, Jesus can take your impossible health conditions and make it more possible. This is called a Miracle. A miracle is an event understandable by nature, scientific laws, or an unlikely event. Some non-Christian medical doctors are uncertain what has taken placed during a miracle thru some prayer warrior at the hospital bed side of near death friend, very injured love one, or very sick person. Our Lord Jesus is the Doctors of all doctors for He has the healing power thru His healing hands. In the Bible, there are many points of healing contacts for believing people to use on other people: such as using anointing oil and laying of hands. Even a prayer cloth from a preacher is helpful for that healing power. I feel much better when my church Pastor anointed me with oil and the laying of hands by those faithful church members. With faith as a small mustard seed you can expect a Miracle to happen. Be praising the Lord for any healing miracles. Our Lord Jesus will take you from the valley of your health conditions to the very healing miracles mountain top.

Years ago Rev. Oral Roberts went around the world with the healing power from God by laying his hands on the blind, cripple, and the sick. His son Richard Roberts has taken over from his father the healing power ministry, he has TV program call The Place for Miracles. Several years ago while living in Indiana, my family watch Rev. Ernest Angley with his healing power ministry alive on TV from the Grace Cathedral located in Akron, Ohio. I have watch by TV the

700 Club with Pat Robertson or his son Gordon Robertson by the Word of Knowledge, the results God's healing power reaching out for someone, somewhere. It happening to me October 2022 receiving the healing-power for my asthma lungs. Hallelujah! I believe in those healing power miracles for they come from our Heavenly Father. Our Lord Jesus perform many healings and miracles in his time and He still doing those powerful healing miracles today and all the tomorrows yet to come. What a blessing from our God with those many healings and those powerful miracles.

> If any one of you is sick? Call on the Church
> elders to pray in faith by using the anointment
> of oil in the name of the Lord. The Lord will
> make that person well.
> (James 5:14)

We must stay healthy by regular check-ups with our dentist and the family doctor. A good healthy program is the real must for yourself and your family. Your body and mind always give you advance warning signs of what is wrongs with your body, like the early signs of strokes or heart attacks. Always check blood pressure, blood test results, have cancer screening, diabetes testing, and watch your weight. Always use your common senses calling 911 for that urgent medical help of going to the nearest hospital. Each person or family member must keep in shape by daily exercise and walking, eat chicken or fish with fruit and vegetables, watch your weight not being overweight or obesity, drink 8 glasses of water daily with limit alcohol, good night sleep of eight hours, cutout drugs and smoking, manage stress, and start using vitamins. According to AARP that sex is healthy as it decreased anxiety, depression, reduce heart attacks, and stress. Always keep your body and mind active and busy each day. For good mind power start with daily Bible study time and read two or three good books each month. Extra health advice regarding heart attack symptoms are usually much less obvious for women than men, be sure staying healthy and being wise. My free good health opinion for everyone is the following: Stay young in your body, mind, and soul; always be useful for your God's purpose in your life journey. Start out with pleasant Top of the Morning with your Lord Jesus by having Bible study time and prayer time as our Lord Jesus will give you that extra strength for those greater hopes. The above health tips will make good New Year resolutions, just do it for your body, mind, and soul. Stay healthy and always be wise, because your Heavenly Father and our Lord Jesus has a plan and purpose for you each day.

> Don't have your body tell your mind what to do, but have your mind tell your body what to do.

There those ole time sayings been around for many years.

> Apple a day keep the doctor away.
> Laughter is the best medicine.

Our Lord Jesus came to give us that abundant life thru His healing hands and the ministry for helping others in need, so keep your faith in Jesus Christ for that abundant life.

I will restore you to health and heal your wounds, declare the Lord.
(Jeremiah 30:17)

Praise the Lord, O my soul and forget not all his benefits, who forgives all your sins and heal all your diseases, who redeem your life from the pit and crowns you with love and compassion, who satisfies your desires with good things so that your youth is renewed like the eagle.
(Psalm 103:2-5)

Do not be wise in your own eyes, fear the Lord and shun evil. This will bring health to your body and nourishment to your bones.
(Proverbs 3:6)

Pleasant words are a honeycomb, sweet to the soul and healing to the bones.
(Proverbs 16:24)

A cheerful heart is good medicine.
(Proverbs 17: 22)

Beloved, I wish above all things that you prosper and be in good health even as your soul prospers.
(3rd Epistle of John)

I pray that you may enjoy good health and that all may go well with you, even as your soul is getting along well.
(3 John 1:2)

Over the years there has been many major changes in medical and mental care for people in America, more than 90 per cent of modern medicine practiced today did not exist in the year 1950. We have more specialized physicians and nurses, modern up to date hospitals, nursing homes, and rehabilitation centers than ever. Since the baby boomers are getting older and now retiring, there will be a greater demand for better and greater health care. The few months of the year 2020, I had twelve chemo treatments at Cookeville Cancer Center for colon cancer. For the final results after rehab care as of August 2020, I am cancer free for that healing blessing, what a great wonderful Wow feeling. God blessings to all the medical doctors and nurses at this Cancer Center and the hospital rehab center for those health needs. When your love ones are in a hospital, nursing home, and a rehab center; they are in good hands with the best educated and trained physicians and nurses with the helpful staff on duty. I know for sure, I been there and done all that. You are in good hands with Lord Jesus, The Great Physician, still makes house calls for all your medical and mental needs. With that faithful prayer for any physical or mental needs, the great Healer is always there with His healing hands.

When I go to places like hospitals, nursing homes, and rehabilitation centers to visit, always take time to pray and talk with any sick person. Just listen what they are saying to you, most of the time there is a prayer request. Always take time to visit with any lonesome older age person for its always nice to be nice and being a good neighbor. Any faithful Christian has a mission for others, the final results there is double blessing for them and yourself. Recalling one time going to visit a friend at NHC nursing home by going down the hallway to her room, there was a lady in the hallway in a wheelchair holding her doll so I stop to talk few minutes and pray for her. Coming back from my visit, the nurse on duty in the hallway told me these words "You made that lady in the wheelchair holding her doll very happy by giving her a smile which was the first since being a patent here." The results of that NHC visit it became a 4-Way Stop of happiness for the lady in the wheelchair with her doll-baby, my friend, the nurse on duty, and myself. What a nice 4-Way Stop experience that day by showing kindness and being nice.

Few years ago, there was this children's Christian TV program called "Mr. Rogers Neighborhood." Rev. Fred Rogers came out to greed the young children and those older people by singing "It's a beautiful day in the neighborhood, won't you be my neighbor." Seeing him with his sweater, sitting in his easy chair putting on his house slippers, and talking his mild soft voice making you feel welcome at his TV Neighborhood Home.

There is a good neighbor Bible story of the Good Samaritan. Jesus wants everyone become just like this faithful good Samaritan. We touch lives with a nice visit or being helpful by showing genuine love and compassion to those older friend or neighbor. Sing to them "Won't you be my Neighbor." Franklin Graham, son of Billy Graham, has an outstanding Christian project known as Samaritan Purse. The purpose of this caring special project providing necessary items and medical care with spiritual prayers to encourage and uplift those hurting people. The old Bible saying, treat others like you like be treated. Jesus touch lives, and as His followers, we must do likewise. How might Jesus touch your heart today?

Love the Lord your God with all your heart, and with all your soul, and with all your strength.
(Deuteronomy 6:5)

For I command you today to love the Lord your God, to walk in his ways, his commands, and the Lord your God will bless you.
(Deuteronomy 30:16)

Love the Lord your God with all your heart and with all your soul and with all your strength and with all your mind, and your neighbor as yourself.
(Luke 10:27)

A man was going from Jerusalem to Jericho, when he fell in the hands of robbers. They stripped him of his clothes, beat him and went away, leaving him half dead. A priest happened to be going down the same road and when he saw the man, he passed by on the other side. A Levite, when he came to the place and saw him, passed by on the other side.
But a Samaritan as he traveled, came where the man was and when he saw him, he took pity on him. He went to him and bandage his wounds, pouring oil and wine on his wounds. Then put the man on his own donkey, took him to an inn and care for him.
(Luke 10:30-34)

Very good and perfect gift is from above
coming down from the Father of the heavenly
lights.
(James 1:17)

Our God in heaven is always there for His children to
give us that protective shield for our living peace and daily
strength as we face the sins of this darkness world.

The Lord is my strength and my shield; my
heart trusts in him, and I am helped.
My heart leaps for joy and I give thanks to
him in song.
(Psalm 28:7)

Grace and peace to you from God our Father
and from the Lord Jesus Christ.
(Romans 1:7)

But the fruit of the Spirit is love, joy, peace, long
suffering, kindness, goodness, faithfulness,
gentleness, self-control.
Against such things there is no law.
(Galatians 5:22-23)

My God shall supply all your needs according
to his glorious riches in glory by Christ Jesus.
(Philippians 4:19)

For this reason, make every effort to said
to your faith, goodness; and to goodness,
knowledge; and to knowledge, self-control,

and to self-control, perseverance; and to
perseverance; godliness, and to godliness;
brotherly kindness, love.
(2 Peter 1:5-7)

IT TAKES TWO, GOD and YOU for Jesus the Healer
has Love for You.

FOUR

Our Love Story

On this subject IT TAKES TWO, GOD and YOU, let me tell you this short story of what happen and how I met my second wife. My first wife died with colon cancer the year 1993, she was fifty-two years old. We were married for thirty-two wonderful years by having two faithful handsome sons and faithful lovely daughter. I was single over six years and feeling very lonely. One day as I as walking in my neighborhood with my dog, Sunshine. I prayed for a lady come into my life.

> Oh God, I come to you in Jesus's name that you sent me a lady to come into my life. Lord Jesus, this is what I want from you: Christian lady, that is attractive, caring, kind, medium build, retired, about same age as me, and like to travel.
> I will accept her family as she accepts my family.
> Thank you Lord Jesus hearing my prayer.

I always went to the Cookeville Library couple times each week to read the Wall Street Journal and other various business articles. This time I picked up the Nashville newspaper, The Tennessean, and as I was going through the paper to the business section. There in front of me were two full pages with a titled "IT TAKES TWO"—one full page single men looking for women and one full page single women looking for men. As I was looking at those single people's ads, I said to myself "I can do that," so I mailed an ad to that paper, The Tennessean.

About three days later, when I got back home from shopping, there was a message on my phone. The phone message said "Saw your ad in the paper, I believe that we have something in common. Please call me." That night I called that number, Nancy and I talk about our background and our family over ninety minutes. She lived over hundred miles away in Bellevue, Tennessee, and was a retired nurse. For few years with her husband and two daughters, they lived in Putnam County, Indiana, the same county where I was born. Her husband died of cancer eighteen years before we met, she was more than ready to start a new relationship with a faithful man.

We met in my hometown of Cookeville, Tennessee as she came here two or three times each month to visit with her mother-in-law who lived in a senior living community. We had lunch together and talk more about our self and our family. We dated for one year and wrote daily love letters and visit each other often. I always wondered what my mailman and her mailwoman were thinking as they delivered those love letters each work day of the week.

The good news is that our families were all for our relationship. We got married that Sunday morning after church services on July 4, 1999 at her United Methodist Church in Bellevue. We were much alike, easy going, and never had any disagreements. We took few yearly small trips visiting family and friends in other states. We always took one big trip each year going to various places including Alaska, some USA states, southeastern and southwestern Canada, five countries of Europe, Ireland, and Scotland. We both got involved doing our family tree research by making trips to different cemeteries and libraries for our information. That was the main reason we were making those trip to Ireland and Scotland, for that is where both our families came from many years ago. Thankful doing my family tree research as I ended up doing my dad of the Robertson family which they came from Scotland and my mom family from Germany, this information being pass on to my children and other family members. Today's advancement by obtaining family research can be founded faster and helpful by using the internet and smart phones.

Yes, our God in heaven heard our prayers. I know for sure that He heard and answer my prayer requests. Nancy's dreams, hopes, and prayers was answer by coming true as well. Our God in heaven turned out to be very good matchmaker, for we had an outstanding marriage of twelve years. She died March 2011 with heart condition, at the age of seventy-six. Both my marriage was super great while they lasted. Thank you, my Lord for all the blessings in my two marriage.

For that long term marriage and special kind of marriage is that of Herbert Fisher and his wife Zelmyra, they been married just under 87 years when he died the age of 105 years old in the year 2011. It's based upon God's Blessing for that long lasting and outstanding Love for each other.

Looking for a faithful soul mate for your marriage to last life time? God is still a very good matchmaker. It happened to me with my two wife and it will happen with your own life by having that wonderful marriage of many blessings. Pray in Jesus name, just asked and you will receive that special soul mate to come into your life. The good news during our life journey, no request is too small or too large for our Heavenly Father. For the good news our Heavenly Father is always there for anyone, anytime of day or night, and anywhere you might be.

Just extra reminder the amazing things what the Lord has already done in my life with my wonderful two marriages, He will do the same with your life for that wonderful marriage. The good news is that our Heavenly Father is not done doing those amazing things. Keep looking up for our God is always there.

IT TAKES TWO, GOD and YOU, just pray for your future true love.

FIVE

Future Planning For
Your Love Ones

This chapter I will share with you some pointers to choose the proper care and places for your aging love ones. This include the following: in-home care, assisted living center for seniors, nursing homes, and funeral future planning. For those older love ones, it is important making plans regarding their health care. In-home care offers the ability to stay in your own home as the aging continue. Your love ones will be with their family and friends for those daily and weekly phone calls or visits. Many in-home care providers offer many range of care from: companionship, doing errands, housekeeping, receiving mail, preparing meals, and both medical and personal care. Maybe your love ones have declining mental status like dementia or Alzheimer which will require additional care, it be wise getting advice from their primary care physician what to do. Once you have select the right provider for your love ones, they will receive proper comfort, welcome companionship, and wonder love.

Assisted senior living centers help residents continue to live an active lifestyle in a comfortable, cost-effective settings that offer many conveniences. Accommodations of these living centers can range from luxurious, detached cottages to cozy apartments. These centers offer medical care by skilled nurses, activity programs, exercise rooms, private dining rooms with good food, and sitting rooms. Choosing an assisted living facility is about finding the right combination to bring comfort and care for your love ones. These senior living centers want their residents feel welcome at their new home. I know for sure at my age of eighty-nine years old, because I been living in assisted center at Heritage Pointe Senior Community of Cookeville, Tennessee for the last few years. Living here it's like living and seeing God's nature wonder land, come see for yourselves. Because this assisted center surrounded by many hills and woods, small stream flowing into small water falls, seeing many birds and wild turkeys, playful squirrels, and at times a deer or two. Living here I am keeping busy by having Bible study ach week, my lady friend and I take time each day visit those special people with dementia or Alzheimer and those shut in people that live here. Always take time to pray for anyone. During those months of hard times with COVID-19 without any those shut-downs, I held some Sunday church services.

A well-chosen nursing home facility will have a huge impact on your loved one. It is best for the family members take extra time to research and visit those nursing homes before you sent your loved one to their new home. Take a tour to check for clues regarding: activities, cleanliness of the building and rooms, clean and proper dress-code of residence, enough skilled nurses and staff, availability of rehabilitative care like occupational and physical therapy, and are visitors welcome any time. Most of important bring your loved one on the last tour, you want that person feel comfortable and having peace of heart and mind in their new living place.

A well plan funeral can prevent your family members from having to make number of decisions at a time when they are confused and sorry of losing their loved one. Family members have enough on their minds dealing with grief with making important decision in a very short of time. According to some experts there are an average fifty decisions to make when arranging a funeral. Take time to visit the local funeral director of making sure you have covered all your basics in your funeral planning. I have done all these with my own funeral arrangements, all is paid in full with no worries on my family. I have made plans with my family and the church pastor for my funeral. For I want my funeral as a church services with several Bible verses and gospel songs with an alter call for healing, prayers of needs, and salvation for anyone in need. Follow by military honor guards, presentation the American flag to my family. Let us sing together that good old Gospel song:

"I'll Fly Away."

> Some glad morning, when life is over, I'll will
> fly away
> To a home on God's celestial shore, I'll will
> fly away
> I'll fly away, O glory, I'll fly away. When I die
> in the morning,
> Hallelujah, by and by, I'll fly away.

At this time want to share the importance regarding the comfort for the dying and the forgotten. Please take extra time each week to visit your love ones by making them feel that you still care and love them. Mostly celebrated birthdays by sharing time togetherness with cards, decorative cupcakes, and flowers plus singing happy birthday. Also, share those happy family times of past years and being together for those special holidays like New Year day, Easter, 4th July, Thanksgiving Day and Christmas. Take extra time honor those brave and proud veterans mostly on Veterans Day with a hand shake and a sharp salute. The local American Legion is doing an outstanding job of visiting with Veterans. I will challenge and encouraged local church pastors and their members become volunteers visits those lonely ones in assisted living centers and nursing homes. It will become a double blessing for you and that love one. It's always nice to be nice.

IT TAKES TWO, GOD and YOU so plan wisely for your family future.

SIX

Wake-Up Call For America

For some of you over the age of sixty-five, you will recall some of these events that took place in America. Let's take a look those past years together. All Christians must pray and work together with our church for making America greater again by having better Christ-like morals and having less sinful ways. For this to happen will take greater faith, more hope, and wonderful love thru our Lord Jesus Christ. It will take a greater wake-up calling from our Heavenly Father by having those ole fashion fire-up spiritual preaching revival come across our America. For sure the political Democrat Party (D Party) and the GOP on Capitol Hill is not the answer, most of the time they are the problem. It will take the Word of God with the full Love of Jesus to solve the problems facing America and rest of this darkness old world. As we go forward in the next several years, let's be spiritual building up our great America.

Just look what took place in America back in the 1960's, the 1970's, and even up to the present time of this twenty-first century, we are seeing declining Christian morals and a broken America. Many decades later we are now reaping what we had been sowing. The U.S. Supreme Court took away the Bible and prayer out our school houses and the court houses, approved abortions by killing millions unborn babies, and now they have approved same-sex marriage. The federal government want men and women use the same rest rooms and locker rooms in some public buildings. Oh my God, what is next that those political people on Capitol Hill will think of next to increase sins into this darkness old world?

The big questions why our schools have become the "blackboard jungle" of America with greater violent actions? Some students just don't care anymore and not wanting learning the three R's. Our education system is facing many unreal conditions: student usage of alcohol and drugs, both bullying and sexual assaulted cases in schools, and students carry knives and guns with shooting and killing in schools and colleges. In America each month thousands of school students are physically assaulted, many bully cases are not even reported. Some school teachers are now allowed carry guns for safety of their students and for themselves. Most schools and colleges have security guards or security devices for safety and security. For several months there in Chicago and other cities, teachers were walking out of their schools demanding better working conditions. The years 2021-2022-2023 our country seeing disagreements between parents and teacher's union of how and what is being taught. What is next for those students and teacher's union is the big unknown? It looks like the American school system has turned into a big battleground nightmare. The days of the one-room schoolhouses are gone forever, those were the good ole days for learning the three R's and Bible principles. Under these absurd conditions we must work together making a better education system. Otherwise, there will be shortage of teachers, maybe it's already happen now. We must and need put our God, the Bible, and prayer back into our schools and colleges. Also, all students should be learning more about our America's history and the real principles of our America regarding the Declaration of Independence and the American Constitution with its blessing Amendments, which will be most helpful. No wonder there is a bigger increased of children going to Christian schools and for home schooling for that faithful sound education. Tax money must be applied for all Christian schools and for home schoolings at the same level for public schooling. Over twenty years ago our high school of academic study was rank number one in the world, now maybe closer to the bottom? If we don't make faithful changes with our education system, it will be blowing in the wind.

The American education system should be making major changes at the high school, trade-vocation school, and junior college levels by providing skill job training programs to keep jobs here on the home front. The colleges and universities across our nation must work better/smater in controlling the cost of higher education. When it takes more than four years or about five years to obtain BA or BS degree from any college or university, it's do due to poor management at the college level. It's time to organize the number of credit hours and offer the necessary courses at the right time for students to graduate on time or less than four years. Coming home to be discharge from the U.S. 8th Army Head Quarters with the 21th Finance located in Seoul Korea. I took my GI Bill and got a BS Degree in Accounting from Ball State University, Muncie, Indiana which I graduated the class of 1960. What has happened in the last sixty plus years when I got that degree in three years including summer school. It takes a good education, greater faith, and hard work to be successful in this competitive business world. This is a major "Wake-up Call America," before it's too late for the future of our country which is based upon good sound education and hard work.

The American education system should learn from Hillsdale College state of Michigan pursuing truth and defending our liberty since year 1844 by going forward into the far future. There main outreach goal is defending and teaching with free on line classes of our American's foundation religious heritage, our country freedom and liberty. These kinds of teaching should be applied nationwide to all schools and other colleges across America. Also, thru Hillsdale College has outstanding program by having well-known men and women come on their college campus be talking about various topics that is hurting our America's history. All this information by those speakers is print through the IMPRIMIS publication by this same college. Thank you, President Larry Arnn of Hillsdale College providing this greater outreach education for anyone wanting to learn more about our religious freedom and America's liberty. Our America needs more conservative colleges/universities like Hillsdale College in Michigan and Liberty University in Virginia. We must not forget the principles of the Constitution with its Amendments which is the cornerstone and foundations for our country freedom and liberty established by those faithful Founding Fathers.

President Arnn of Hillsdale College had an excellent speech with the same write-up thru IMPRINIS publication dated January 2022 regarding our twenty-first century education system with the title "The Way Out." With questions why is civics government and American history education is practically banned in America's schools? Also, regarding the broken education system in Loudoun County, Virginia with those very upset parents as they express their feeling with the school board. The big questions why are children being subject to critical of race theory and what is being taught of the distorted istory of America? Also, President Arnn write-up "Education as a Battleground" dated November 2022 with putting children's education first. The big honest question what is being taught to your children in other schools across America? Now more than ever for more quality education and less radical from the far-lift. We are a great country and we need to make sure our children have the greatest education opportunities. More than any other time, now is the time to fight back with a good knock-out punched for sure we don't want the far-left be in education control.

One more write up in IMPRINIS dated May 2022 that Disney the most famous children's entertainment corporation in history, maybe the likes of Donald Duck, Mickey Mouse, and Snow White are gone forever. The management of Disney opposition of the new bill banning discussions of gender identity in elementary classrooms up to the fourth grade. This bill "Don't Say Gay" was approved and signed by Florida Governor DeSantis and the state legislature, plus the approval bigger majority of Floridians. We must be aggressive of togetherness for our children's Christion education.

Nearly 50 years ago, Hillsdale College began publishing IMPRINIS as part of a nationwide extension of its education mission. Their mission for year 2022 is to expand the impact of IMPRINIS by increasing its circulation at free cost to more than 6.5 million business and households. Your financial support will be most helpful for this outreach in this vital time for our nation with our main purpose is "Pursuing Truth and Defending Liberty."

Planned Parenthood is our country largest abortion provider for killing unborn babies which is financial and mostly supported by the far-left D Party. Because Planned Parenthood has become the "Holocaust of America," we must educate all young women regarding about abortion with its harmful health's side effects. There are married couples wanting and more willing adopted those babies so they can become faithful happy parents. Maybe the U.S. Supreme Court could not solve the question when life begins. Just ask any doctor or a mother, they will tell this higher justice court that human life begins at conception. The years from 1973 to the year 2023, the estimated number over 63 million unborn babies being killed or being murdered because of abortion. Has the people of America forgotten about God's Ten Commandments, one of them is "You shall not murder?" Another questions for the "so call justice system" of our America, what is the real legal difference killing unborn babies or murder unborn babies? We must appoint more conservative federal judges and vote for government leaders who will protect the rights for pro-life and who will support the value of these unborn babies. The Forty-fifth President Donald J. Trump and his Vice President Mike Pence are for pro-life and this president has appointed hundreds conservative faithful federal judges. The sad news is that the far-left Forty-sixth President Biden, Vice President Harris, and the far-left D Party are not pro-life, the final end results more unborn babies will be killed or murdered.

For several years mostly the year 2022 there has been a bigger pro-life movement by those faithful ladies for pro-life events as the March for Life. Tens of thousands people were there January 2022 for the pro-life rally, "Equality Begins in the Womb, for the 49th annual March for Life at the Nation Capitol by marching toward the Supreme Court. These annual March of Life always been held one day before the Roe-Wade anniversary, now those marching ladies having growing optimism victory feelings. Otherwise, they keep on marching until Roe-Wade is overrule. Nice write-up in The Stand magazine dated January/February 2022 of the ladies from Bryan, Texas came together formed a pro-life movement known as 40 Days for Life. Since 2004, along with one million volunteers, FDFL has ministered in 64 countries, witnessed over 19,500 babies saved, and seen 114 facilities close their doors. With many God Blessings to all these pro-life marching Ladies.

After receiving God's wake-up for pro-life calling, the Supreme Court has indicated it will allow states to impose tighter restriction on abortion. Even some states of America are taken stronger standing-up for pro-life. Such as the state of Mississippi and other states with their latest law prohibit nearly all abortions after the 15th week of pregnancy. Also, the state of Texas passed pro-life law known as Texas Heartbeat Act which bans abortions after baby's heartbeat as early six weeks old. December 2021 Texas passed a law no mail-order abortion drugs be allowed in that state. Other states reporting there more abortion drugs usage with less abortion surgery being done causing several abortion clinics closing doors for good. Any physician, health care person, and abortion facility should be charged with criminal offense facing prison time for doing abortion. After nearly fifty years later, the U.S. Supreme Court considers the ruling regarding of Roe-Wade for this could the most significant abortion cases in history. It came true as June 2022 with the approval by the Supreme Court for this become a big pro-life turn around victory. They passed the buck of R-W down to each state governor.

However, there might be a dark cloud that be coming, the Forty-sixth President will be appointing Supreme Court Judges. Will they be conservative judges which we mostly need or they be more like the far-left socialism minded judges? The conservative judges will take our country forward into greatness for future generation yet to come, while the far-left socialism judges will take our country backward into many darker unknowns. Hopeful the Church with the backing of those faithful prayer warriors will be praying for knowledge, understanding, and wisdom from our Heavenly Father for these future Supreme Judges and those federal judges. The bad news as the Spring 2022 some evil people for abortion rights on purpose have damage with paint the outside walls mostly those Catholic Churches. Also, there are active protesting women carrying signs for abortion and reproductive rights with the theme "Bans Off Our Bodies." It might be those darker days ahead between the Supreme Court and those people using those over counter abortion pills.

My questions and concerns "Where was the Church and the Prayer Warriors during these trouble times of evil conditions?" This is a "wake-up call" regarding our religious liberty. Now the time for the Church with their Pastors take a greater stand-up approached against the sins of this dark world. For all God believing pastors be preaching what your church need be hearing regarding God's Words from the Bible. What will the Heavenly Father have to will say to those lukewarm churches with those water down sermons from those pastors? Total repentance is the only answer for those lukewarm churches. Now our country need God's wake-up calling for a fire-up Holy Spirit ole fashion spiritual revival for that total repentance. Prayer time for America for there is Living Power in Prayer for there Living Power in Jesus.

Early Spring 2019 our America were facing the Caravan invasion of thousands people from Central America wanting to live in America. Some of them were evil ones bring in drugs to sell in our America for they were not welcome to stay, this situation would increase violent crime and increase the homeless madness. However, the legal people were welcome to stay in America. President Trump want build a longer wall on the southern border of Mexico to stop this madness of unwanted non-legal people. The D Party in the U.S. Congress refused provide necessary financial funds for this most needed wall project. However, American President Trump got financial money from other government funds help build this most needed longer wall across the Mexico border. Year 2020 our Forty-fifth President Trump put an end of this Caravan madness by sending those unwanted people back to their home country.

Now for the bad or sad news during the first month in office, this far-left Forty-sixth President approval with his Vice President, and rest the far-left D Party administration opened wider the southern border between Mexico and our country. That same year 2021 people with children by the hundreds of thousands start coming into our America. The full year 2021-2022 under this far-left administration is still welcome these unwanted people, estimated 12 million coming across the southern Mexico border from several countries. Without Title 42 it will become out of control madness for years 2023-Jan 2025 additional estimated increasing over 25 million. Was this far-left administration main purpose these people become the future voters for the D Party, possible yes? This Caravan condition is now out of control without any fast solution by the Biden Administration. He pushed this heavy burden on the backs of the mayors and state governors. Which created major crises for all these states regarding food, housing condition, medical care, and schooling. This could increase the COVID, for sure increase major crime with the drug-smuggling market, terrorism, human trafficking, and more homeless people population.

Our America is facing so many major unreal problems as the following: the honest or dishonest 2020 National Presidential Election, for those years 2021 into 2024 seeing the out of control crime with shootings and killings, wildfires in the Western states, unsolved homeless population across America, high inflation, the broken global supply chain crisis, the unfaithful media, shoplifting with stores closing, any future pandemics. The very worst condition by this far-left administration wanting the terrible far-left Socialism system for America. This will be the final end of America as we once known it.

O my God, what will this far-left D Party leadership be creating with the next sinful conditions that our country be facing?

May 2020 Minneapolis white police officer holding his knee on the neck of black man, George Floyd, for more than eight minutes as he struggling to breathe. The final results after this deadly crime, it became like an avalanche of uncontrolled demonstration of anger, destruction, shooting with killing, and looting through-out many cities across America. Next, our country with people were damage many statues of patriotic heroes which is part of our American history, this will become lost history for future generation of Americans. Even in southern California people destroying Christian statues and burning various churches. Many D Party city mayors and state governors across America ignored these evil sad conditions and now they are wanting cutting-back their local police force. At the same time with those hateful reasons our brave and faithful hard-working police officers are being shot and killed leaving behind their love ones. Satan the devil and his demons are causing all these evil minded rioters by controlling the far-left movement. With these evil conditions what will happened to our religious freedom and liberty? Times like these our Prayers of Faith in God will give our country that most needed greater hope.

The final results of these unrest conditions our citizens across America are becoming less safe. People of America are seeing alive on TV these out control looting like those of Crash and Carry crimes and shoplifting causing closure in various retail stores. The Windy City of Chicago is rated the most violent murder America's city, the year 2021 there were almost 800 murders, the highest in 25 years. People living in that crime city are afraid getting out of their homes or walking the streets in the darkness of the night. Sadly, major cities across America, crime have soared without any punishment because unfaithful justice system and dishonest bail reform. Defunding our local police is not the answer for it will created more crime problems that be facing America.

These unrest conditions facing our America during this twenty-first century with so many big questions being asked "Why is this happen without any honest rightful answer." The big question being asked will this far-left minded Forty-sixth president with his far-left administration be able solving today problems facing our country with these: out-control caravan, more violent crime, higher inflation, racial concerns, any future unknown conditions? The real answer by this president 4 years (2021 to 2024) administration might be blowing in the wind. With those conditions facing the people of America, only faithful prayers will be the only answer as God will provide emotional and spiritual healing for our country with faithful greater leadership in the mid-term election year 2022 and the presidential election year 2024. Now is the time for building up America, not burning down our great country.

The higher courts of our country have forgotten the big issued of same-sex married couples, that is two gay men or two women known as known as lesbians wanting adopted children. What mental-physical side effect for those children's lives? According to the Bible regarding same-sex marriage, God does not approve of this sin. Now our country is facing issue that of transgender, some men wanting become a woman and some women wanting become a man. Somehow schools, college, business places, and work places will have to come up a working plan for these people using rest rooms and taken showers. Our God in heaven is the only judge for a faithful America not any unfaithful judges making wrongful decisions. Our Heavenly Father is in charge for a Christian faithful marriage relationship that is one man as the husband and one woman as his wife. They in turn will be able having children which will created a faithful and happy family relationship. Thank goodness we are all God's children by putting God first in our lives.

> Shameful lusts as women exchange natural relations for unnatural ones. In the same way the men also abandoned natural relations with women and were inflamed for one other. Men committed indecent acts with other men, and received in themselves the dues penalty for their perversion.
> (Romans 1:26-27)

With so many years of racial concerns that cause many deep hurts in our country, now is the time for corrections and improvements. It must start with your house going to the church house from there the courthouse of justice, school house, and all the way to the White House. Several years ago at one of Billy Graham crusades in NYC, He said these words "God in heaven is for all people whatever your color or race." The Rev. Dr. Martin Luther King Jr. with the same opinion open the services with a prayer at that same crusade. We are seeing the years 2021 and 2022, maybe future years, as several people carry posters and signs with words Black Life Matter. According to our Heavenly Father and our Lord Jesus Christ, that All-Lives Matter, for we are God's children. Which in turn will make a more faithful and greater America-Life-Matter. As faithful Brothers and Sister in Christ we must always believe in these powerful words: In God We Trust in order that God Will Bless America. The big question for these uncertain times, when will they learn, will they ever learn? We must treat each person with the love of Jesus, for the Bible states treating other people like you like be treated just like the Bible parable of the Good Samaritan. During these twenty-first century uncertain conditions, the Billy Graham Rapid Response Team and the Samaritan Purse are always there to provide spiritual prayers with the Word of God and the love of Jesus for those hurting people. Only Jesus Christ's love is the only answer during these political and racial darkness times facing our country.

Over the years there has been many outstanding black men and women in our country, these are some of the first of their working careers:

Joe Louis known as the Brown Bomber became the World Heavy Weight Boxing Champion.

The great Jackie Robinson outstanding baseball player with the Brooklyn Dodgers, 1955 World Series Champion Hall of Fame.

Sidney Poitier the outstanding Hollywood movie star with many great movies, these are just a few of them:

"Lilies of the Field" "In the Heat of the Night," "To Sir, With Love," and "Guess Who's Coming to Dinner," ¶ Rev. Rev. Dr. Martin Luther King Jr outstanding Civil Rights Leader movement with his "I Have a Dream."

Barack Obama as the Forty-fourth President of two terms.

Kamala Harris Lady Vice President with the Forty-sixth President.

Several years ago the musical trio of Peter, Paul, and Mary had two great freedom songs. First song "We Shall Overcome" with words "How many roads must a man walk before you call him a man." Those uncertain times during the 1960's into the 1970's or even today, this song has been described as a civil rights anthem. The other great song by this same musical trio is "Where Have All the Flowers Gone?" with some words of "Where have all the flowers gone, blowing in the wind. When will they learn, when they ever learn?"

It's a good question during these the political and racial times that are facing our America today. My concern for America during these unknown times what will happen next into the far-off twenty-first century years with many unknown answers regarding when will they learn, when they ever learn?

"It's Me Again, Lord" a song written in 1964 by Dottie Rambo as our America facing many unknowns. Yes, Lord, It's America Again, during this twenty-first century as our country have several questions with fewer answers. We must become Prayer Warriors with our Church by kneeling in prayer to our Heavenly Father to answer our prayers for that greater blessing of America. During the 2016 National Presidential Election, the people of our country prayed and voted for new leadership of making America Greater Again.

The final results for America from that election, America's Forty-fifth President Donald J. Trump taken the GOP all the way to victory. My personal viewpoint for this victory prior to the 2016 national election that Franklin Graham, the son of Billy Graham, went all fifty state Capitols by having prayer time and revival time for our country have repentance. Again for the same reason on September 2020 Franklin Graham held the "Last Call for America" Prayer March at our National Capitol for the 2020 National Presidential Election. We need another Prayer March across our America for better leadership on Capitol Hill, hopeful this will come true with mid-term 2022 and 2024 national elections.

During his first four years in office this president made appointment three conservative faithful U.S. Supreme Court Judges and appointed some three hundred conservative faithful federal judges. These right appointments will make a big difference of where our America will be heading into the far future of this twenty-first century. With many faithful prayers our Heavenly Father will bless any American President, the Vice President, the Cabinet Members, the U.S. Supreme Court Judges, and those conservative federal judges. All America's business and government leaders must be blessed with the love of Jesus in their hearts and minds with knowledge, understanding, and wisdom in order have greater USA. Just pray in Jesus name that our business and government leaders have the same knowledge and wisdom just like King Solomon. This King Solomon, the son of King David, asked God for faithful knowledge to lead his people of Israel. With King Solomon's faith, that prayer was granted and he became the wisest man who ever lived because the source of his knowledge, understanding, and wisdom all came from the Heavenly God. We want this same kind of faithfulness for our business leaders and the leaders of mayors, state governors, and federal government by taking our America forward with greatness.

Many people in this dark unknown world are lacking that total faithfulness what is best for their own lives. The sight is limited by what people see ahead for them. Our Heavenly Father with His Son, our Lord Jesus, are always there to give us advice, encouragement, and the needed help in our Christian walk. It will take your faith and positive purpose prayers for your future goals and those many needs so plan wisely. Now the time come to the aid of our country with those daily Bible study times, those faithful daily prayers, and by going church each week. The final results of pursuing God's wisdom, all believing Christians will become wiser in our lifelong pursuit. Our Heavenly Father has great plans and a greater purpose for each person for He will provide all the necessary knowledge and wisdom for your big dreams and those bigger goals that can last a life time.

> The fear of the Lord is the beginning of knowledge.
> (Proverbs 1:7)

> Get wisdom, get understanding; do not forget my words or swerve from them.
> (Proverbs 4:5)

> Wisdom is supreme; therefore get wisdom.
> Though it cost all you have, get understanding.
> (Proverbs 4:7)

God has no problems, only plans.
Corrie ten Boom

During good and hard times facing our great country, the hard working people would always roll up their sleeves and got their hand dirty with that good ole fashion hard work this what it takes greatness America.

> Lazy hands make a man poor, but diligent hands bring wealth.
> (Proverbs 10:4)

> My heart took delight in all my work, and this was my reward for my labor.
> (Ecclesiastes 2: 10)

> Person must work, doing something useful with his own hands, that he may have something to share with those in need.
> (Ephesians 4: 28)

America was once the most religious and God fearing country in the world, again we must change becoming God-believing country. We must keep our big dreams, greater hopes, and those outstanding vision come more alive. We want our God, the Bible, the prayers, and the Ten Commandments back again across our America in our schoolhouses, our courthouse of justice, the House of Congress, and all the way to the White House. The best place to start is with your house by going to your church house every Sunday. It's time to stand firm and tall for your rights, that is the freedom of the press, the freedom of religion, and the freedom of speech.

This is no time for the Church with their Prayer Warriors be sitting on their hands, lets speak up and stand up for those freedom rights. Let's start right Now, by taken those changes to God in prayer for a faithful repentance come across our land. It only takes God and just one church, God and just one person with our togetherness for total repentance with those words in God We Trust in order that God Bless America again.

> When the foundation is destroyed, what can
> the righteous do?
> (Psalm 11:3)

> Woe to those call evil good and good evil, who
> put darkness for light and light for darkness,
> who put bitter for sweet and sweet for better.
> (Isaiah 5:20)

IT TAKES TWO, GOD and YOU with the Church and positive powerful prayers making greater powerful America.¶

¶

SEVEN

Hurting America

The next three chapters I will be praying for you, your family, our America with the business and government leaders of our country, and those brave and proud military that are still serving our country for our freedoms and liberty, I'm a Korea War veteran that served my America years ago. Also, what has happened to our beloved country over the years. Third, God's calling for America always be faithful partner with Israel and His people.

Let's stand firm and tall in what our Founding Fathers of 1776 believed in. They had dreams, faith, hopes, and a greater vision for our country. Those faithful heroes were seeking what was over the next hills, those mountains, and beyond the valleys. It was their vision that enable them to see the invisible that we will have greater America. Those Founding Fathers must have hear the voice of God through their dreams, prayers, vision, and thru the Words of the Bible. Our America have been the lighthouse for the world, but now our America has fallen into the world's darkness of dishonest and sinful. We want a country be under God with faithful leaders believing in the Ten Commandments and the Constitution of the United States with those faithful powerful Amendments. America let us start Now by making those better changes in our Christian beliefs and morals. Otherwise, there will not be a decent tomorrow for our children and their children. If we don't change those evil ways, we will be seeing our America blowing in the wind, being gone forever. My faithful Americans, let's put those dreams, faith, hopes, and more visions into action right Now during this twenty-first century. So we have our America going forward with greatness again. We must never forget where our America came from with these mighty words, "In God We Trust" in order that God Will Bless our America. My Brothers and Sisters in Christ the only answers is thru the Words of the Bible and the love of our Lord Jesus with your faith and many powerful purpose prayers. If the people of this world, mostly those of our America, will only turn away from their sinful ways and humble themselves as faithful prayer warriors with those praying hands reaching toward heaven. Then the people of our America will hear the voice of the Heavenly Father for His blessing and healing our America.

> If my people, who are called by my name, will
> humble themselves and pray and seek my face
> and turn from their wicked ways, then will I
> will hear from heaven and heal their land,
> (2 Chronicles 7: 14)

> Now faith is being sure of what we hope for
> and certain of what we do not see.

Hebrew 11: 1)

President Thomas Jefferson once said many years ago, "The best government is that which governs least." It's a crying shame that the politicians in Washington D.C. in this twenty-first century don't have the faith, vision, and wisdom of our Founding Fathers. Any American President and Members of Congress must understand not bigger government but better government is best for the working blue collar workers and the white collar workers of America. They are the only hard working people that roll up their shirt sleeves and got their hands dirty for a true working America. Political people there on Capitol Hill in Washington take a lesson that hard work is good for the body, mind, and soul, let's be working together. President Donald J. Trump was not a political Washington person which is good for our country for he has the Christian business background and experience of making proper and rightful business decisions by taken our country forward into greatest. His promise in the 2016 National Presidential Election rebuild and restore our America's economy with greatness by lower income taxes for small business, corporations, and the working people of America; secure our borders, having stronger military, pro-life for the unborn, and religious freedom. He made those promise and he kept those promises. Vice President Mike Pence was a successful business minded Indiana Governor, he balanced that state budget by lower taxes while in office for the Hoosier State. His outstanding Christian leadership created better and more Indiana jobs. This president and his vice president were good working team for those wonderful four years. Thank you Lord for given us those faithful

Christian men and women that has the proper leadership that understand these uncertain times facing America and know how to fixed them. One of the biggest problem for any American President is that of making both sides of U.S. Congress, D Party and GOP, working together as a team. It takes good sportsmanship and teamwork for any winning organization such as a sports team to succeed. Big government take a lesson on how to become a true winner, it only takes good sportsmanship and teamwork.

Take a lesson the values of good sportsmanship and teamwork from the late legendary head basketball coach of UCLA, Coach John Wooden. He was an All American basketball player at Perdue University of West Lafayette, Indiana. This great college coach led his team to ten NCAA college basketball national championships in twelve years, seven of them in a row. Those records may never be broken by any coach. Coach John Wooden was selected national basketball coach of the year six times. He had the faith, love, and wisdom of how to lead and win.

Now is the time for all Americans start saying "Enough is enough" to our big fat federal government. For sure America needs better federal government not a far-left bigger one. As faithful Christians, we must always be praying for our great America and their leaders. We need more faithful leadership in our business working places, the local, state, and federal government; all working together for a greater America. Such faithful person will stand up for what he and she believes for getting our nation's economy or any unrest conditions facing our country back on the recovery road. Just only believe with faithful prayers that our God will bless and heal America again. With God's blessing and thank goodness we had over the last 248 years, 1776-2024, many faithful outstanding Presidents and their administration leaded out America back to greatness. It took those faithful presidents with their strong backbone and greater leadership abilities during those hard times facing our country of depressions, recessions, and those war years.

It's not just the budget deficit that Uncle Sam concerns about there on Capitol Hill in Washington. It's also the trade deficit which is ballooning. During the year 2020 President Trump, Vice President Pence, and their Cabinet members work hard for America having successful trade agreements with worldwide countries mostly with Canada, China, and Mexico. Year 2022 largest trade deficit on record.

IT TAKES TWO, GOD and YOU, we have faithful Presidents with conservative Judges.

*There are lots of unnecessary spending by our big government, our national debt including one trillion dollars annual interest more than 35.5 trillion dollars year-end 2024 and much higher in future years. Uncle Sam is not able to help anymore with his bad back and he is financial broke. *This not including the D Party bigger financial spending (anyone wild guest for sure more red ink trillion dollars) for the terrible Coronavirus and the Forty-sixth President economy programs. Consisting the Semiconductor Bill and the Inflation Reduction Act and others as the far-left Congress passed both these very unwise costly bills. Excessive spending bills of several trillion dollars has created a 40-year high inflation rate for 2022 into 2024.

"The GOP Calvary coming to save America" by Larry Kudlow, the economic wizard, for Fox Business News. The 2024 Presidential Election, the GOP must win changing our

America from Biden's D Party Socialism back to America's Capitalism.

Charley Wilson, one of President Eisenhower's top business minded Cabinet members of those yesterday years ago of the 1950's with his statements "What good for General Motors is good for the country." This is not true anymore in this twenty-first century business world. Now day of the yeas 2021-2022-2023, people are getting paid by staying home. Those people are saying "What is Work." Build in America and Buy in America only by putting people back to work. Then there was that old time advice years ago "never buy a car build on a Monday or a Friday." But your new car dealer will tell you his cars are built only on Tuesday, Wednesday, and Thursday.

The growth of these two twin deficit, America will be borrowing more money from foreign countries which is mostly from China. As of year 2020 these countries own about 45 per cent of America's Treasury debt. Borrowing from foreign countries means paying higher interest on this growing outstanding debt which will never be paid in cash. It's a shame that our country has to borrow more money from foreign countries or print more red ink paper money so those political D Party and the GOP in Washington D.C. can spend or waist more of our hard working money. Sometime in the near future, those countries be wanting their loan-money be paid back in total. Because of our red ink dollars, they wanting be paid only by taken our prime America's farm lands or prime real estate for payments. Is this time for America to wake up?

March 2020 our America and other worldwide countries were attacked with COVID-19 from the Chinese Communist

Party, it caught the world's countries off guard. It caused all the whole wide world countries come to their knees in prayer. This invisible unknown virus came from our number one enemy Communist Red China to attacked on purpose mostly our America. This communist country under its evil leadership with their main and only goal become the number one economic and military world power country. Which in some future time this will become true for a short time in years. However, God has other plans regarding for this evil country, be the Battle of Armageddon, the War of all wars.

The last nine months of year 2020 and both years 2021 and 2022, this COVID-19 has changed the ways we live, work, and worship. All people must do their share of duty-call by wearing their mast all the time and getting all those vaccines. The good news with advanced medical research by corporations like Johnson & Johnson, Eli Lilly, and Pfizer, they created rapid development effective vaccines with fast on time delivery. At the same time doctors with trained nurses become more medical informed plus obtaining on time delivery those proper medical devices and supplies. Many business organizations in America and the federal government will be better prepared next time for any future pandemics. God answer our prayers for this most rapid medical research bring closer end to this COVID-19. Let's Praise the Lord for this much needed winning victory against this terrible world invisible virus. Also, let's give credit for the outstanding leadership of both President Trump and Vice President Pence with their economy working team and mostly the medical team for their medical care leadership.

Some information regarding this COVID-19 with the write-up IMPRIMIS publication by Hillsdale College dated

October 2020. It is based upon the outstanding study by Dr. Jay Bhattacharya, Professor of Medicine of Stanford University. He claims there are more health harm by this virus because of those lock-downs. These are some of his study: The result of these lock-downs many parents had stopped bring their children into medical clinics for immunization against child-hood related disease cases. Over 135,000 more people around the world will starve because of the economy lockdowns. Many people are more afraid of this COVID-19, that they stop taken their cancer chemo treatments. There is more risk of this virus for older people over age of seventy, be sure that you take those two vaccines plus the two boosters. The COVID-19 fatality rate is in the neighbor of 0.2 percent, higher of 0.4 percent for many older people. COVID-19 is beyond the people of America, but not Beyond God. Let's become more Faithful and less fearful regarding this terrible disease.

The Center Disease Control (CDC) reported greater increase in anxiety, depression, and suicidal among young adults. The outstanding write up by President Larry Arnn of Hillsdale College with the title "The Way Out" of the IMPRIMIS publication dated January 2022. The state of Michigan enforced these lock-downs causing local small business owners being crippled or destroy. This the story of one of them: Regarding the results of two lock-downs at this family owned restaurant a 30-year dinner known as the Spangler's Family Restaurant of Jonesville, Michigan that employed 20 employees were facing with the wheels of bureaucracy repeatedly by the health department and that of the licensing authorities. Thankful this faithful owner did not give up for he was in control not the government with many prayers and the backing of the local towns it became winning victory.

The final terrible results from this most terrible COVID-19, that millions of jobs were lost causing many unemployed people facing difficult financial hard times. Thousands small or mid-sized business places have to closed or may never open again under present ownership, while others are mostly struggling just to stay open for business. Because of on-line trading with Amazon and the COVID-19 effects saw two old timers K-Mart and Sears were closing their doors for good, may never return again. With so many unknowns who is next, maybe your company? Because of this COVID-19 that hit America with many hardships that most people having greater negative feeling toward China. Because of China's economic and military evil minded president, America's unfavorable views for that country of 60 percent which is up from 47 percent from year 2018. China should be accountable for these terrible COVID-19 conditions. The question is HOW, maybe reduce our borrowing debt to that country.

The Summer of 2021 came another round of the horrible deathly virus COVID -19 Delta. Alert warnings came from Center Disease Control (CDC) that people must have two vaccines plus two boosters. Maybe, like the yearly flu shots will this booster may be required yearly? We have battling this deadly COVID-19 and Delta pandemic that has killed more than 1 million Americans as of Spring 2022, mostly during the year 2021. The CDC done everything in their power with the latest information to protect the public for their health care. Beware America and rest of whole wide world countries of the any coming deadly pandemics for any year, beyond years. Let's become more Faithful and less fearful with all these pandemics facing the whole wide world.

If you have any or most of these conditions get medical care immediately, stay home until you feel better. Otherwise, wear your mask in public places and always use hand sanitizer or wash hands with soap-water for 20 seconds. The latest Data as of January 2022 has indicate that OMICRON remains dangerous for those people being not vaccinated, who are 13 times more likely to be hospitalized with the disease than those fully vaccinated. These conditions are creating hardship at hospitals with soaring cases across America with exhausted medical staff as many health-care workers have quite or some of them has the virus by staying home. Hospitals cannot operate under these conditions of being under-staff. It a big must for people get all those vaccines, if you are not feeling well, please stay home. We don't know how bad any kind of pandemics will become for those future years, let's be safe not being sorry.

Those four years under the leadership of this far-left 46th President with his Vice President and rest of the far-left D Party administration has cause many hardships on America not able solved so many many unknown conditions regarding: the wide open border of caravan, bank crises, increasing violent crime, their economy programs with increased spending by trillion dollars, out of control inflation of financial hardship, if any future pandemics, and any war-like conditions from those evil minded leaders with China, Iran, North Korea, and Russia. The good old days for full economy under President Trump leadership maybe gone forever or it be many years later for good economy comeback.

Who getting richer with Biden wanting electric cars-trucks while China building batteries? Must stop Chins buying more America's farmlands.

With the booming economy of future years under President Trump administration showing a very low inflation rate less 2.0 percent and a very strong Gross National Product (GNP) estimated of 4.0 percent with lower unemployment rate which the results of this president lower tax programs of 2017. For the real terrible news there on Capitol Hill under far-left President Biden Administration with the backing of the far-left D Party wanting increased spending several trillion dollars which caused greater higher inflation-higher taxation which will damage our country's economy. With so-many unknowns? The Federal Reserve will have their hands busy by slowing down or stopping this out-control higher inflation with no end in sight for consumers peaked of 9.1 percent, hopeful goal 2.0 percent. All those booming economy good times under President Trump administration will come faster ending as the Federal Reserve has plans of increasing interest rates during both years 2022/2023. Those higher interest rates must be rightful timing, not too fast or too much. The latest survey years 2022 into 2024, that 85 per cent of families and farmers believe they are facing financial hard times. Mainly because with the following conditions: future soaring high inflation of food, record high for regular gas and diesel fuel, higher interest rates causing more expensive borrowing, and future/higher taxation programs. Which will create harder financial times for small business owners, corporations, families and farmers with coming recession fears with estimate GNP 2.5 by year end 2023, not better for the year 2024 with GNP 2.5 even less for 2025. Several Economic experts forecasting of a short/soft recession are rising by year 2024 as the Federal Reserve began cutting interest rates years maybe 2024 for sure 2025/2026. Serious downturn will cause major layoffs and higher the unemployment rate of some 4.25 percent. This far-left D Party on Capitol Hill created these terrible conditions without any fast fixing solutions. These are estimates numbers. Faithful Prayers is the only answer for these uncertain times. Heavenly Father always in full control by taken those deep fears into deeper Faith.

> To get our nation back on their feet, we must
> get on our knees.
> Billy Graham

Always keep in mind those famous words few years ago by President John F. Kennedy: "Ask not what your country can do for you, ask what you can do for your country." Also, that famous address by Rev. Dr. Martin Luther King Jr. "I Have a Dream." Those two speeches by both those two great leaders encouraged our America for many years and more years yet to come. My fellow Americans and the future generation what can you do for your country and do you have a dream? Don't let your dreams, hopes, and future visions be blowing in the wind. Those faithful Founding Fathers of our America had good viewpoints for our country growth by building and laying the cornerstones and foundation for America's greatness. The big question for any American President, Vice President, and mostly with the Members of Congress is what can do for your country? All it takes by getting on your knees in order that our nation be back on its feet. Always be thankful that our God will provide any president and administration with greater knowledge, understanding, and wisdom. Let's win togetherness of making America Greater Again. Your promise President Trump and Vice President Pence during the 2016 election year for making America greater again and it is still the Promise of all promises. It has become promises made and promises kept all because this president got on his knees in prayer by getting this nation back on its feet.

I Have a Dream for that young Martin Luther King Jr. must had started in those early years when he went to his Baptist Church there in Atlantic. Later, attending Morehouse College where he saw the Holy Spirit Light as God preparing him for those future dreams. He got on his knees in prayer to his Heavenly Father to become the Peace Maker for his America and for his own people that he so loved. With those daily talks and walks with his Lord, he became the new faithful fisher of men for his country and for his people. From the valley all the way the mountain top lets be serving God by moving hate into the Love for all mankind.

Our daily prayers become powerful force for our America with the return of a godly country. All churches across our country should take few minutes each Sunday morning, Sunday and Wednesday evening services to pray for our country and our leaders that we have world peace. In this twenty-first century these are difficult and trouble times facing America and her people. When we pray with faith in Jesus Name, God in heaven will answer our daily faithful prayers by blessing and healing our America back to greatness again. Than it will become Hallelujah Times than with those Praising Times.

In my life time of eighty-nine plus years, there been many hard times for America as the Great Depression with those terrible years that took place most of the 1930's. Many people were facing so many unknowns, it all started October 1929 with the Wall Street stock market crash causing many banks, business places, and corporations filing bankruptcy or going out of business. Causing high unemployment with those long soup lines for people without jobs having something to eat. Across America farmers and ranchers were facing bankruptcy or hard times as the dust storms destroying their lively income. Federal government with the helping state Governors came to the rescued under the great leadership of the Thirty-second President Franklin D. Roosevelt with the New Deal programs which became our country economy comeback. For this faithful president it took hard work with teamwork from his administration to restore the faith and confidence of the American people.

After the Great Depression years this fourth term president was facing with another major crisis as America turned again to President Roosevelt. It was that sad Sunday morning December 1941 as air planes from Japan attacked the U.S. naval base of Pearl Harbor in Hawaii. It became breaking shocking news on all radio stations that Sunday afternoon with disbelief people. The following day, this president addressed Congress and next the nation by radio with those words "a date which will live in infamy." Which started World War 11 in the Pacific Islands with the country of Japan. It became bloody and costly long world war across those two oceans. The leadership of both General Eisenhower and General Patton with so many bloodies battles as the Battle of the Bulge and D-Day of Normandy. Which put an end to end to Hitler's supper power when Germany surrender June 1945 and stop his madness killing millions of Jews.

Under the great leadership of President Harry S. Truman continued with the atomic bomb research and development known as the Manhattan Project. It became the very big top secret countdown with the brightest scientific and top military minds in the nation coming together. It took many military man-hours of meetings and those of Truman, Churchill, and Stalin all regarding quick ending this Japan War with the atomic bomb. The arrival at Tinian Island of the USS Indianapolis delivery top secret weapon of the first atomic bomb known as Little Boy, next the arrival by B-29 plane carrying the second atomic bomb known as Fat Man. The very sad news few days later the USS Indianapolis was torpedoed by Japanese submarine causing this naval ship sank to the bottom of the Pacific Ocean, only 319 of the 1200 sailors survived. After two advance warnings, Japan refuse to surrender. The final countdown as atomic bomb, Little Boy, was on B-29 plane name ENOLA GAY heading for Japan under commander Colonel Paul W. Tibbets with his 507th crew. Few days later another B-29 carrying the second atomic bomb, Fat Man, heading for Japan for the final blow. War is Hell!

During this second World War, Americans on the home front prayed, came forward, and work together supporting our U.S. military armed forces. We were buying War Bonds, using ration books and stamps for buying food, gas, and tires, even town people planting victory gardens in their back yards, recycling any kind of metal and rubber products for the war, government reducing the speed limit to 40 mph on highways. Brave, proud, and young men were drafted or volunteer for the military so we still have our freedom and liberty. Many hard-working women went to work in factories across our great land making war goods such as guns, planes, ships, and tanks. They were better known as "Rosie the Riveter." Also, women served in various organization such as the American Red Cross, the USO, and many women enlisted in the armed services as clerks and nurses. The farmers and ranchers of America's heartland were exempted from the military for the sole purpose providing food for the military and the feeding the hometown people across America. Big thank to all the brave and proud military and veterans for serving our country, the people on the home front doing outstanding job, and bless you all for making our America the land for our freedom and liberty.

The early 1950s was a three-year war with North Korea and it was one of America's least popular war. It started as a civil-war between Communist North Korea and the Republic of South Korea. Even this twenty-first century our country facing many unsolved war-like concerns with North Korea's evil leadership. The 1960s it was the war in Vietnam, that was supposed to solve the problem of superpower hostility. It was a war that divided our nation and left scars that are still not healed even today. Because of this war our country was facing trouble times with many protests, riots, and other unrest situations.

Next, that sad morning for America with the Islamic terrorism attacked 9/11/2001 of the Twin Towers in NYC and the Pentagon in Washington D.C. Which cause a long war against both countries of Afghanistan and Iraq. Our country has memory services each September 11th for the 3,000 people were killed. These were fathers and mothers, sons and daughters never be going home again to their family. Those were sad times facing America. Now in this twenty-first century, our America is facing many number one enemies with war-like conditions with Red China, Iran, North Korea, and Russia, and those unknown terrorist countries for future attacks. Summer 2020, our Forty-fifth President Trump, his Vice President Pence, and Cabinet Staff were working together by solving any those war-like conditions. We must have all-powerful military forces under the leadership of a powerful strong President as our Military Commander in Chief for our America's freedom and liberty. Otherwise, a weaker President will be facing with many war-like conditions with those evil minded leaders of Red China, North Korea, and as years 2022-2023 with Russia attacking Ukraine. There is always been time for war and time for peace. Thank goodness there is the full armor of God for our country of safety and security. Whatever the world condition, maybe bad with war like conditions or good with peace, our Lord Jesus Christ is the Prince of Peace.

Seer peace and pursue it.
(Psalm 34:14)

Now may the Lord of peace himself give you
peace at all times in every way.
(1Thessalonians 3:16)

He must turn from evil and do good: he must
seek peace and pursue it.
For the eyes of the Lord are on the righteous
and his ears are attentive to their prayer, but
the face of the Lord is against those who do evil.
(1Peter 3:11-12)

DON W. ROBERTSON

April 2018 was a big four-day event, thousands of patriotic folks came from far and near to traveled to my home town of Cookeville, Tennessee to show their respect to those who died in Vietnam. Also, they came to thank all active duty military members and shake hands with the veterans. It was the Wall that Heals, the 375-foot replica of the Vietnam War Memorial in Washington D.C. It was a must to see and it was. May 28, 2018 as I was watching with my lady friend the special PBS TV program from Washington D.C. of the 150 year anniversary remembering Veterans Memory Day. It was in honor for those military men and women that served with outstanding courage and mostly to those brave and proud who sacrificed for our great America.

We are facing in this world financial and political unknown conditions and it will not get better anytime soon, regardless of what America does or doesn't do. We have seen many major financial ups and downs, war like conditions, and several other hardship conditions. But the people of America would always roll up their shirt sleeves, got their hands dirty, and they went to work so that your children and grandchildren will have greater and more safe America. Those faithful hard working Americans wanting our nation be one in Victory and true Faithful Winner. As always it takes greater faith with many prayers and lots of hard work to make all this come true. Over several years our America been real bless with our much stronger Christian background and those faithful stronger believes. We were founded as a Christian nation by our Founding Fathers of 1776. Those Founding Fathers came forward with strong approved and signed The Declaration of Independence July 4,1776. Few years later approval of the Constitution of the United States with its faithful many Amendments.

We must keep those dreams, hopes, and the greater vision alive for future generations yet to come with those faithful prayers all in Jesus name. Our America started with the thirteen colonies and now a great and mighty nation of fifty states. As of July 4, 2024 which will be 248 years ago, we are a country of faithful Americans that still believe in those words "IN GOD WE TRUST." Those same Founding Fathers in 1787 approved the Electoral College for our national presidential election. That each state will have the same equal number of votes, the small and the large states alike. Never should any political D Party or the GOP in Washington D. C. have the power or the right to change our Constitution and its Amendments or removal the Electoral College in order to win in any election. We are truly a Nation for God, in God, and under God.

In a write up in the American Legion Magazine of June 2017, that 57 percent of Americans want the United States to deal with its own problems and let other countries get along the best way they can on their own. This is a bigger change in opinion from the 30 percent in year 2002. The American Legion is one hundred years old as of 2019. This is a great organization honoring our military and help veterans making better transitions. Like so many other Americans, I am a proud Korea War veteran serving my beloved America with honor and proud and belonging the Cookeville American Legion Post 46. The last several years I been financial supporting those great military and veteran organizations such as these:

American Legion, Disable American Veterans, USO for they are over there, we are here, and the Wound Warrior Project.

Over the years many veterans and those brave proud disable ones have been real blessed with the Veterans Affairs (VA) which provided medical and mental care, and for those with special needs in those veteran hospitals. For myself with the GI Bill, I obtained my college education with my accounting degree, paid up life insurance, and now from the VA receiving helpful financial means for my assisted living.

Where I lived at this assisted senior community, Heritage Pointe, there are few old veterans living here. One of them my older friend, Lehman Riggs, machine gunner with the 2nd Infantry Division during the Battle of the Bulge. At one time he was the oldest living World War11 veteran in Putnam County, Tennessee, at age 101 years still being young at heart. As the oldest member of the all-volunteer Veterans Honor Guard by playing "Taps" in ceremonies to more than 1,000 funerals for the deceased military. Memorial Day 2021, this old war horse played his final "Taps" with the Cookeville Veterans Honor Guard. August 2021 he passed away, we will miss you my good old friend. God Blessings all those old time veterans and the brave and proud Fighting Warriors who are now serving with honor for our America's freedom and liberty, their proud families and friends who support them.

The week of February 3rd 2022, American Legion across America observe Four Chaplains Day, named the four military chaplains who gave up their life jackets so others would live after a U-boat torpedoed their transport ship, Dorchester, in the North Atlantic on February, 3rd, 1943. We have four Army chaplains of different faiths all praying in their own way to God asking for help. God answer those prayers as the escort cutter, Comanche, with its crew rescued 93 of 277 survivors. These are the names of those brave four chaplains with their faith: George L. Fox (Methodist), Alexander D. Goode (Jewish), Clark V. Poling ((Reformed), and John P. Washington (Catholic).

During my grade school days of the 1940's into my senior year of 1953 there in Danville, Hendricks County, Indiana even up to the present time of this twenty-first century, I always have respect for our American flag. It shows the sign of hope and strength what our faithful and proud Americans believed in. It hurts my feelings and pride when certain evil unfaithful person or people shows disrespect by burning our flag. So many brave and proud military fighting warriors fought and died for that "Ole Glory Flag." They did this in order all Americans have our freedoms and liberty here in our own country and those other countries around the world. In this twenty-first century there are some chaotic political leaders in our America want do away with the Pledge of Allegiance in schools and various public places. We been saying those words of the Pledge of Allegiance in our schools since 1892. This Must never happen for this is part of our liberty and justice for all.

I feel the same way with any American President and their Department of Defense, that we need a stronger high-tech military for our America. In this uncertain world of this twenty-first century, we need be on guard all the time by having the latest proper military equipment. That is the main reason for any faithful and strong minded Commander in Chief with the approval of the U.S. Congress to increase the military budget each year being better prepared of any terrorist attacked on our country like the one of 9/11. Our military must win over world's number one enemy or some terrorist country. We must always support our military men and women plus our veterans. It was July 2017, which I watch TV Fox News where our Forty-fifth President made a speech in honor the world largest USS Navy aircraft carrier in honor the late President Gerald R. Ford. We are now on the way for a stronger U.S. Navy which is a must against Red China and Russia powerful military. Some political Washington leaders believe that America have become the policemen of the world long enough with our military. One thing in this world is missing that of world peace, it always been that way and always will be in this dark old world. In order have world peace, we need peace of God and peace with God. A powerful military is one which the troops must have good high morale, in that situation they will follow any good military officer in any battle or combat. Our country must have a powerful military with the leadership of a faithful respectable Commander in Chief, that will back up the military with proper aircraft, ships, tanks, and up to date military equipment. It's more possible with the full armor of God for the proper protection of our active military in any battle of heavy war zone. We must be providing good medical care for the active military plus the disable and wounded veterans in those VA hospitals. Just keep up the good moral with good pay and benefits, the fighting military will go all the way to victory for their country. By showing our American spirit for our active military and those proud veterans always take time to shake their hands and with a proud salute to each one.

There were sixteen million Americans, consisting 350,000 women, in the military during World War 11. During this World War General Dwight D. Eisenhower, better known as Ike, made this statement "It's not the size of the dog in the fight, It's the size of the fight in the dog that counts." Wise words by two other World War 11 hero solders that of General George Patton "If everyone is thinking alike, then somebody isn't thinking." Also, before the first wave at Utah Beach the bloody attacked of Normandy (D Day) as commander, General Theodore Roosevelt Jr. stated "Ringside, Hell! We'll be in the Arena"

Today most men between ages 18-24 are not qualified for military duty because following conditions: bad attitudes, drugs, lack of education, and health or mental conditions. In this twenty-first century it has become all volunteer military of both men and women. Our strong military are well combat trained like the special military of the Green Beret, the Top Rangers, and the Navy Seals with their fire-up fight for our freedom and liberty. Our America is the Land for the Free, because of the active brave military and those veterans that fought for our freedom and liberty. For the final war, our Lord Jesus with His Angels and Saints, these are the born again people, will be riding down from heaven on their big white horses for the War of Armageddon. It will be the War of all wars being won by our Lord Jesus with the word of God from His mouth.

> Blessed the peacemakers, for they are called
> sons of God.
> (Matthew 3:9)

According to Vince Lombardi the great winning professional football coach of The Green Bay Packers with fight to win words:

> Solders and professional football players are
> supposed to win.

Winning is not everything. It is the only thing.
To play this game, you must have that fire in you.

There was this head football coach Rockne of Notre Dame given his pep talk in the locker room to the Four Horsemen Fighting Irish. ND won 11 National College Football Championship with these 5 winning coaches: Knute Rockne, Frank Leahy, Ara Parseghian, Dan Devine, and Lou Holtz, for they believe in the size of the fight to be victory champions.

This is great Bible story by using God's victory battle plans for the Israelites with Joshua's leadership in the conquer of Jericho.

> Then the Lord said to Joshua, "See, I have
> delivered Jericho in your hands."
> March with your men once around the city for
> six days. On the seventh day, march around
> the city seven times, with the priests blowing
> the trumpets.
> When you hear them sound a long blast on
> the trumpets, have all the people give a loud
> shout, then the walls of the city will collapse.
> (Joshua 6: 2-5)

There are sadness times in our life time with heart aches by losing a war military family member for it may feel like a heavy wall is enclosing around us. Recalling back during World War 11, families placed a red flag in the living room window for losing a military member. If this sad condition is happening to your family or another family, take those hurting concerns in prayers to the Heavenly Father for His healing power for any those hurting families.

There is another Bible story regarding having the right weapon at the right time. It took place in the Valley of Elah, as the Israelites were fighting the Philistines. The Philistines had their nine footer champion warrior that of Goliath. When the Israelites saw this giant man, they all ran in fear. But God had his own fighting warrior, a small young shepherd boy that of David go out to fight him. David without any sword in his hands, his weapon consisting only five stones and a sling. But God was with him in this battle for David reach into his bag and taking a stone, he slung it with his sling and struck the giant Goliath on the forehead. The stone sank deep into his forehead and he fell face-down on the ground. When the Philistines saw their champion warrior was dead, they turn and ran away of being defected.

Thru prayers, God will provide the necessary Christian spiritual armor for our victory on those front lines battles or those evil terrorist against our America. For battle preparation there are the full armor of God: Belt of truth, the Breastplate of righteousness, the Gospel of peace, the Shield of faith, and the Sword of the Spirit. When we have God on our side, who can be against us. When our Fighting Warriors come marching home, it will be Hallelujah Time and Praising times for America. There is a mighty song written by Sabine Gould:

"Onward, Christian Solders."

> Onward Christian solders! Marching as to war, with the cross of Jesus Going on before.

> The energy, the faith, the devotion which we bring to this endeavor will light our country

and all who serve it, and the glow from that
fire can truly light the world.
President Thomas Jefferson

Let's take pride in our beliefs, we must become more
believing and faithful by having a greater vision for our
America. We want our America that is united, that is
victorious, and is a winning nation. We need go to the Lord
in prayer for our country become that greater world power
country. Let's pray as believers that our loving God will have
mercy and reunited our country again.

The following words having true meaning for our county,
lets share these words to all the people of America:

GOD BLESS AMERICA

God bless America,
Land that I love,
Stand beside her and guide her
Thru the night with a light from above;
From the mountains, to the prairies,
To the oceans white with foam,
God bless America,
My home, sweet home
God bless America,
My home, sweet home.

THE AMERICA'S CREED

I believe in the United States of America as
a government for the people, by the people;
whose just power are derived from the consent

of the governed—a democracy in a republic—a sovereign nation of many sovereign states; a perfect union, one and inseparable; established upon those principals of freedom, equality, justice, and humanity for which American patriots sanctified their lives and fortunes. I therefore believed it is my duty to my country to love it; to support its Constitution; to obey its laws; to respect its flag; and to defend it against all enemies.

Yet even now, "declare the Lord, return to me with your heart."
(Joel 2:12)

If we ever forget that we are One Nation we will go under.
President Ronald Reagan

Looking back those space-age history years, Americans were shock by watching on TV the Challenger disaster, everyone on board were killed. Next was the day when the world stopped with estimated 530 million people around the world watch by TV, the CBS News and listened the voice of Walter Cronkite of the first man landing on the moon. July 2019 was the 50th anniversary of the Apollo 11 mission with astronauts Glenn Armstrong and Buzz Aldrin became the first men to walk on the moon, on board was Mike Collins in charge of space ship controls. "It became one small step for man, one giant leap for mankind." We have come long ways from those days of the 1940's comic books with space-heroes of Flash Gordon and Buck Rogers in their space ships.

The Forty-fifth President Donald J. Trump wants our county become the leader in the outer space program. Going to Mars is the new vision of the future for America with one giant leap for mankind. This president wants this space age become our new military branch like the other five military branches.

Let us as believing Christians start praying, that our God will forgive those sinful ways and heal our country again. Our America needs a mighty revival come across our America bring back greater faith, more hope, and lasting love with the Word of God and the Love of Jesus. We want a nation that has Victory in Jesus, a nation full with the Holy Spirit for a faithful America. Just believe and pray—this is the only way for our God can bless and heal our nation again.

May 2, 2022, was the 70th Annual National Day of Prayer. It was created in 1952 by joint resolution of the U.S. Congress and signed into law by President Harry S. Truman. If the Pilgrims, both President Abe Lincoln and President Franklin D. Roosevelt and so many other presidents had never under estimated the power of prayer. There was only one U.S. President that did not approved the National Day of Prayer. That was the Forty-fourth President and that was very sad day for our country. Each year for the National Day of Prayer at the Cookeville, Putnam County courthouse, the theme "Exalt the Lord," prayers were voiced for our churches with their pastors, the economy, our education, your families, God's Israel, our government leaders, the madness media, our brave military, and the proud veterans. It's a must that our America have its National Day of Prayer each year with total Repentance for our country. People of our America still believing those words "In God We Trust," with greater faithful prayers for our country and its people that God Will Bless America. We must stand together in believing those great words as our Heavenly Father is always there respond to our needs.

God has blessed many world nations over the years, our America and God's Holy land of Israel are the most blessed of them all. The average life time of the world's greatest civilizations from the beginning of history has been about 200 years. We don't want our America become like those past-years unfaithful nations. Just like that old saying: "What goes around, comes around." Maybe it is true. The following words are the 200 years of civilization history:

> From bondage to spiritual faith.
> From spiritual faith to great courage.
> From great courage to liberty.
> From liberty to abundance.
> From abundance selfishness.
> From selfishness to complacency.
> From complacency to apathy.
> From apathy to dependency.
> From dependency back again to bondage.

Where is America in the above, maybe between selfishness and complacency? Maybe much closer to apathy, because some unbelieving people in our country just don't care anymore for they only care for themselves. According to year 2020 Harris Poll that almost half college age students would prefer to live in a socialist country's economy. What will happen to our America as the far-left D Party with the current President and his Vice President wanting Socialism be in control. Beware the danger of the Socialism rocky road, later it will become the next no way out Communism super highway. If and when this happen our America will never be the same again, losing all our great freedoms as Big Government be in total control. Our country greatness is based upon the powerful big three C's: Christianity of our Lord Jesus Christ, strong Capitalism, and the Constitution of the United States with those faithful Amendments. Beware, with total control Socialism all those freedoms be blowing in the wind, never return again. When America loses its faithful leadership regarding the above most important and powerful big three C's, it will not survive. When a house is divided it will not stand, that is true with a divided country. From the days of our Founding Fathers to this twenty-first century, our country will be 250 years old as of July 4, 2026 which is above the 200 years average for the history of all civilizations.

God has blessed America from the days of the Pilgrims coming to their new world over 400 years ago to the very present of this new twenty-first century. Under these uncertain times or those terrible unfaithful conditions facing our America, for sure there a greater need for a faithful stable church in this unstable world. Our America and rest the whole wide world need be hearing the crying voice of our Heavenly Father for a great revival awakening.

> Freedom is never more than one generation away from extinction.
> President Ronald Reagan

IT TAKE TWO, GOD and YOU for making Greater and Stronger America.

EIGHT

Capitalism For Greater America

Our America needs more believing Christians and faithful prayer warriors. My dear Brothers and Sisters in Christ get on your knees and prayed mostly for our America with their leaders, our military and veterans, your family and your friends. We are living in these unknown trouble times for we don't know what tomorrow holds. Just put your faith in God for He's got the whole wide world in His hands. He got the tiny little baby, myself, you, and your family all in His caring hands. Our Heavenly Father and His Son, our Lord Jesus, are always there for everyone and the future generation yet to come.

Lord Jesus is the one that controls those darker uncertain storms of our daily lives that maybe blowing in today and those tomorrows yet to come. We serve a Son of God who will step out of the bow of our vessel during a stormy day and say "Peace, Be Still." God is that bridge over those deep trouble waters of our daily lives for He got the whole wide world in His hands. With our Heavenly

Father and His Son always there in our life journey, by taking us from the valley of many unknowns all the way to the glorious victory mountain top. Make sure for each day just feed your faith with the love of Jesus and He starve your doubts.

> No eye has seen, no ear has heard, no mind has conceived what God has prepared for those who love him."
> But God has revealed to us by his Spirit.
> (1Corinthians 2: 9-10)

Be sure have those daily Bible reading and study time with your family and friends. The Bible is your most precious possession in your home and for your lives. Each person or family member should share God's Holy Word with other believers as well those who need to know our Jesus as their own personal Savior. This is no time to be quiet about our Lord Jesus Christ being the world Savior for Salvation. The end times or last days of this church age is now, the Rapture of His Church could happened this very hour or could happened in our life time during this twenty-first century. We need a good ole fashion fire-up revival come across our country like a mighty whirlwind to bring back God's Ten Commandments to placed them in the heart of all mankind. We must put our faith, hope, and true love in God's hands for He love everyone, so those will love him. You are my people and I will be your God for I will not leave you. For that lasting hope just come as you are for that greater loving hope in our Lord Jesus for He is with us each day and those days of evermore.

The Lord is good to those whose hope is in
him, to the one who seek him.
Lamentations 3:25)

The year 1965 President Dwight D. Eisenhower sign
measure making the words "In God We Trust" for our
America motto. Few years ago, the pastor and members of
the Colonial View Baptist Church put up on the Putnam
County courthouse of Cookeville on each four sides in big
letters IN GOD WE TRUST. Every courthouse in America
should have those same words, have the pastor and members
of your church speak up and stand up and be sure that it's
done. The believing people of your community will be real
proud as it become your big show and tell event. It's true in
my home town, come see for yourself.

We must always believe that the Bible is the only word of
God. President Ronald Reagan had the faith in the year 1983
signed into law with the Act of Congress making it the "Year
of the Bible." This wild unknown world of this twenty-first
century that we are living in, every year should be the "Year
of the Bible." We need more Bible believing people with faith
and righteousness in our business world also in our local,
state, and federal government for making America greater.

Commit your way to the Lord; trust in him
and he will do this;
He will make you righteousness shine like
the dawn, the justice of your cause like the
noonday sun.
(Psalm 37:5-6)

For the word of God is living and active. Sharper than any double-edged sword, it penetrates even to dividing soul and spirit, joints and narrow; it judges the thoughts and attitudes of the heart.
(Hebrews 4:12)

We must be sowing faith seeds in our hearts for a greater and stronger America. Let's put our hands to the plow and sow faith seeds in black rich soil so plow deep and wide that those faith seeds will have deeper roots. Sowing faith seeds in your live will provide a greater marriage relationship and a greater family relationship which in turn make a greater and lasting stronger America. By sowing those faith seeds always be expecting many miracles of blessing. We must obey His Ten Commandments each day by cutting out our daily sins of life, then the good Lord will give us His "Showers of Blessing," that will last forever. It takes a lot of faith and courage for people to speak up and stand up for theirs believes. Just remember having more Faith of deeper roots, there will be less fear.

You can become a faithful wise sower by listen to the voice of God as you study the words of the Bible, always be sowing seeds of faith in black rich soil that they have deep roots produce harvest crop hundred times. Just like the Bible parable of The Sower as told by Jesus. The seeds are the word of God, some people listen good and believe the word of God in their body, heart, and soul. Become one of those faithful sowers!

He who works his land will have abundance
food, but the one chases fantasies will have his
fill of poverty.
(Proverbs 28:18)

A farmer went out to sow his seeds. As he
was scattering seeds some fell on rocky places
where it had shallow soil. When the sun came
up the plants were scorched because they had
no roots.
Other seeds fell among thorns, which grew up
and choked the plants.
Still other seeds feel on good soil, where it
produced a crop—a hundred, sixty, or thirty
times which was sown.
Matthew 13:3-8)

We are engaged in a spiritual warfare every minute, every
hour, and every day, so be-aware of Satan the devil and his
evil demons. Our Heavenly Father wants all people become
Christians so take a firm stand by putting on the full Armor of
God and be ready to win against those evil ones with the Sword
of the Spirit which is the word of God. Let your Bible become
the Armor of God for that living peace. We will be marching
off with victory being in God's army with our Lord Jesus.

The Lord your God is with you. He is mighty
to save.
He will take great delight in you, he will quiet you
with love, he will rejoice over you with singing.
(Zephaniah 3:17)

I have told you these things, so that in me you may have peace. In this world you will have trouble. But take heart! I have overcome the world.
(John 16:33)

Therefore put on the full armor of God, so that when the day of evil comes, you may be able to stand your ground, and after you have done everything, to stand.
Stand firm then, with your belt of truth buckled around your waist, with the breastplate of righteousness in place, and with your feet fitted with the readiness that comes from the gospel of peace. In addition to all this, take up the shield of faith, with which you can extinguish all the flaming arrows of the evil one.
Take up the helmet of salvation and the sword of the Spirit, which is the word of God.
(Ephesians 6: 13-17)

Is our God up in Heaven telling us something or trying to shake us up, that we are in the last days of sorrows? Our own country is going thru uncertain trouble times regarding these conditions: wide open southern Mexico border, increase violent crimes, financial crisis, terrible disasters, shortage baby formula, millions of homeless people, 40 years high inflation, mass killings, opioid epidemic, broken supply chain, global warming, and many rumors of wars.

I will high-light one of the above sad conditions facing our land, the issue of mass shooting with killing: October

2017 the worst mass killing in America's history took place at outdoor country music concert in Las Vegas as the lone gunman killing sixty people and wounded over five hundred people. Spring 2022 gunman using AK-15 assault rifle with the mass shooting massacre of 10 black people in a Buffalo super-market. Again May 2022 mass shooting slaughter at Robb Elementary School of Uvalde, Texas, 19 fourth grade children and 2 teachers all killed. May 2023 6 killings at Covenant Elementary Presbyterian Christian School of Nashville. According to The Washington Post write-up: Since the Columbine High massacre in 1999 to May 2022, more than 311,000 children at 331 schools have been exposed to gun violence within their schools. For greater protection and safety at schools, we need more police officers and proper safety devices. These mass shooting with killing of anger and hate done by mental disturbed teen-age boys or young men, not by teen age girls or women. Parents if you have mental disturbed teen-ager or young man still living at home, become more aware by getting proper medical or mental help. That same be-aware advice with those school friends and teachers what is happening around you for your help is most needed.

It's unbelievable the many mass shooting and killing in churches, schools, colleges, and work places are taken place over the world, being total out of control. Weapons by themselves don't kill, people are influence by the evil Satan the devil which kills. In my life time of ninety plus years, I have never seen so much human wickedness of hated, terrorism, and violence. We must believe in the opinions of the NRA by having guns in the homes across America for our own protection and safety. God has given us His spiritual weapons which is the Full Armor of God. Wear those daily by putting on your Helmet of Salvation to give you living peace of your mind. Put on your Breastplate of Rightness having a heart of love, and the Belt of Truth being honest and truthful. Below is one of our rights the American Constitution with its Amendments that was ratified in the year December 1791 by our Founding Fathers. Be-aware of any far-left political person or some evil people want make major changes to the Constitution and its Amendments.

The right of the people to keep and bear Arms shall not be infringed.

2nd Amendment of the USA Constitution.

Operation Blessing from CBN the 700 Club always come to the rescued with chaplain spiritual supports, food, medical supplies, and water helping those hurting people in any areas of major floods and storms disasters. Also, from the Billy Graham Rapid Response Team (IBG-RRT) sent crisis-trained chaplains to offer spiritual support anytime-anywhere like those hurting people in Las Vegas, Uvalde, Nashville's Covenant School, and those people of various disasters. Those well trained chaplains offered loving care and spiritual comfort to many hurting individuals and families. They did it in the name of Jesus Christ bring greater hope, more joy, and much love back into their lives. Our Heavenly God created the heavenly lights as our Lord Jesus become the lighthouse of the world for He will start with those people of dark hopes and bring greater hopes from heaven. God and His Son, our Lord Jesus Christ, will bless everyone with forever faith, greater hope, lasting joy, and much love that will last a lifetime.

We are seeing falling away from the truth of God's word, even in the church. All people of America must and need be hearing with your ears and seeing with your eyes regarding this out-control decreasing Christian morals and the terrible sins of this dark evil world, for we are living in the same ways of the world. Our Heavenly Father is calling for repentance of our sinful lives. For that wake-up calling for total repentance, we must and need that ole fashion fire-up Holy Spirit filled revival come across our country. As God's children it's time get on our knees in prayer for this kind of revival. We need to rekindle those old revival fires and keep them burning all the time. Pray that our Heavenly Father will provide that greater spiritual hunger revival, the spiritual hunger of God's Word, and spiritual thirst for the Love of Jesus.

> The days are coming, declare the Sovereign
> God, when I will send a famine through the
> land-not a famine of food or a thirst for water,
> but a famine of hearing the words of the Lord.
> (Amos 8:11)

Our America needs more faithful men and women with good leadership in both the business world and in our local, state, and federal government. My fellow Americans our big government is not the solution to our country financial problems at times they are the real problem. Because having bigger government is the problem that is facing us each month and each year. The last several years there has been political party split in our U.S. Congress which lacking good and sound working agreement with any American President. It has become doing nothing Congress, split down the middle between the political D Party and the GOP. They get their annual salary no matter what they do or don't do. Where there is no vision for any country, the people will perish because any country that is divided cannot stand. With many faithful prayers to our Heavenly Father, He will bless our America's leaders and give them a humble and kinder heart that they have greater love for our country.

Please Note. I'm using the TV media's opinion of which political D Party or GOP being the honest or dishonest in the 2020 Presidential National Election. This 2020 presidential election was seeing the D Party presidential candidate wanting a wrongful socialism America with a bigger federal government. With bigger socialism government, it will become The Big Brother will be in total control of everyone and everything. People of America will be seeing less of our great freedoms: freedoms of the press, religion, and speech. Faithful America's voters must vote for those D Party candidates or those GOP candidates that has the best principles for a greater powerful America. Majority of people voted mostly for their own political party not so much as the candidate's good or bad principles. That was the way it was by going back to the years that their parents and grandparents voting either being right or wrong for greater America. What's the future of the coming years for America with the far-left Forty-sixth President and his Vice President with the backing of the far-left D Party? The first month and rest the year 2021 in office with his power, this president reversed mostly the right things for a greater America that the Forty-fifth President did for our country during his term in office. This Forty-sixth President and his Vice President with the backing of the D Party increased spending for their Inflation Reduction Act economy programs by several trillion dollars which cause greater inflation by hurting our country economic growth and causing financial hardship for those hard working family. Also, they opened wilder the Mexico border for the Central America caravan as those unwanted people bring-in more crime and drugs into our USA. Some other future plans by the far-left D Party: defunding the local police force, taking away our rights having guns for our protection and safety, more money for Planned Parenthood by killing more unborn babies, and increase taxation for small business, corporations, and the working people. Are these reason why this far-left D Party have 70 percent negative rating? These unbelievable promises if carry out will ruined our America's economy by causing mild-recession with unknown housing and stock market. Under these conditions it will become just like those terrible years of the Forty-fourth President with his Vice President, which is now the Forty-sixth President. The final result will be several big giant steps backward for America's economy and decreased our standard of living.

Under the leadership of this Forty-sixth President, and his Vice President with the strong backing of the far-left D Party, America will be heading toward Socialism. Causing people be totally dependent upon big government by having total-control of everyone and everything. In some future time, Satan the devil with the Antichrist and the false prophet be in total control of whole wide world Socialism Party. The Antichrist, as Big Brother, be in control of one world socialism government. The false prophet be in control world's economic system of buying and selling. If all this happened for our America, we may never see our Christian life the same again. Will this the beginning of the end for our America?

Now, is the right time by bring this overwhelming America government back where it belongs under the control of the working people of America. This far-left Forty-sixth President and his far-left D Party administration has no solutions of the problems that they had created. Can and Will this president turn his presidency around for the good of our country? This has become a big wake-up calling from the hard working people, that this president with his D Party administration must make major changes for the best of our country. Now more than ever the church with their prayer warriors must be in prayer for our business and government leaders for a faithful and greater America. One thing for sure our Heavenly Father is still in control not any socialism party. With those faithful prayers our Heavenly Father with his Son, our Lord Jesus, will bless and heal our America.

> We know that in all things God works for the
> good of those who love him, have been called
> according to his purpose.
> (Romans 8:28)

According to some TV media people been reporting that this 2020 National Presidential Election was dishonest with fraud and possible financial backing the D Party of buying votes. These TV media are claiming wrongful ballot counting, missing GOP mail-in ballots, and the wrongful computer program being used in some twenty-eight states. The final votes of Electoral College showing the elect Joe Biden became the Forty-sixth President with California

Senator Kamala Harris as his Vice President. The final results the far-left D Party has won this 2020 National Presidential Election. The bigger question by all faithful Americans and the GOP's viewpoints has Satan the devil and his demons taken total control of the far-left D Party so they have greater political and economy control for Socialism?

Jesus and all those faithful Christians will cry and wept for our America by going from Capitalism the best system for the working people to Socialism for Big Brother be in total control of everyone and everything. Your grandchildren will be asking many questions:

"Grandfather tell us about the good ole days when men had many freedoms and now there is none." What is your answer?

Not socialism, more Lady Liberty Capitalism.

> A truthful witness gives honest testimony, but
> a false witness tells lies.
> (Proverbs 12: 17)

> These are the times that try men's soul
> Thomas Paine

This Forty-fifth President Trump with the faithful backing of the GOP still stand for the capitalism system of making America even greater. Capitalism is the only working system for the blue collar working people, white collar working people, for your working family, and for greater working America. It means more jobs, more opportunities, and more prosperity. The following are some major issues that President Trump and Vice President Pence stood for:

promote Patriotic education, job security, protect pro-life, save our religious freedom, stronger military, lower taxes, and build longer wall on the southern border. President Trump has improved medical care for both our brave and proud military and the veterans. This American President has protected our country by his stand up against those evil minded leaders in various countries. President Trump's outstanding victory of foreign policy that of Israel/UAE Middle East the working deal for world peace. This proves that this Forty-Fifth President and his Vice President are great friends for Israel and their people, and their Prime Minister, Benjamin Netanyahu. The foundation for greater America is based upon the three C's which are the these:

Christian faith with our Lord Jesus Christ, Capitalism for greater stronger America, and the America Constitution with its Amendments.

Seeing the unpleasant 2020 presidential election results, President Trump and Vice President Pence had high hopes for their victory and for America's victory. Will this prior president be running again in the 2024 National Presidential Election as being the GOP top choice? Many things will happen between today and the 2022 mid-year election and the 2024 National Presidential Election.

There were more than 75 million votes mostly Christians people voted in that 2020 national election more than ever for any president. Some 50 million Christians did not vote in that election, what would the final results been if they had voted? Always stand-up for your principles and rights; its God-given privilege and responsibility. This is our great America don't anyone forget or forsake it. We will not back down for our Christian believes.

President Trump, Vice President Pence, and the GOP have not given up the results of this 2020 presidential election for reelection. The main reasons being right or wrong for sure the mad media was doing all the so-call delusional talking. There are several bigger question without any rightful smaller answers as former Vice President Biden won this election? There so many questions with-out any answers why twenty-eight states were using this same software computer program? How many lost GOP votes were there for President Trump? President Trump and the faithful GOP voters done their part, next God will do His part.

President Trump and Vice President Pence are leading the charge of making America Great Again. This president has taken actions for improvements for future National Presidential Elections. The U. S. Attorney General Bill Barr under President Administration should have come forward stronger to speak up and stand up with this president for our voting rights. We must Stop any future election fraud or wrongful counting and only legal register people can vote by showing proper photo ID's. It takes faithful leadership making and taking our country to Victory in order our God will take our country to greater Victory. This well done President, his Vice President, and rest the GOP Administration had made promises and all those promises were well kept and working well during those four years of serving our country.

There were many well done presidents, these are just few of them: those presidents of the 1770's into early 1800's like President Washington, President Adams, President Jefferson for they were our America's Founding Fathers, President Lincoln of the mid-1860's with slavery freedom and calming those Civil War years, the presidents of 1930's into 1940's like

President Franklin D. Roosevelt with his New Deal programs solving those depression years and regarding those Infamy World War 11 years, and President Truman for ending that terrible Japan war with the new weapon-atomic bomb, President Eisenhower victorious Army General of World War 11 and president of 1950's regarding cold war tensions with Russia and building the interstate highway system, President Kennedy of 1960's regarding his New Frontier programs building stronger financial economy, President Reagan of the 1980's with the Reagan Revolution boosting the economy by lower taxes, and so many others well done presidents. America must need the backing of the church with faithful prayer warriors for those future presidents that they become well done presidents.

Judicial Watch with their president and his faithful working team supporting and working together with President Trump, Vice President Pence, and the GOP for a faithful honest election. Judicial Watch being the nation's largest and most effective government watch dog. If there were any D Party cover ups and wrongful under the table deals, it might be very hard to find evidence with proof regarding election fraud or any wrongful doings in that 2020 presidential election. Maybe from the GOP view point this has been well organized and plan well by the D Party. If there were any wrongful doings in that 2020 presidential election, we may never know the whole honest truth. In the proper time God will deal with any dishonesty for He is for honestly in government and in our lives.

Results from the Electoral College final vote Congress confirms that formal Vice President Joe Biden become America's Forty-sixth President. Two month after the

November 3rd National Presidential Election President Trump acknowledge his defect and claim "I totally disagree with the outcome of the election, there be orderly transition." February 2022 the Forty-fifth President spoke at large CPAC meeting bring the GOP back to greatness in future elections.

The first two years of 2021/2022 for sure the far-left D Party have total control on Capitol Hill in Washington. However, depending the results of any coming economy conditions or world conditions during the years 2022 to 2024 there will be many major changes on Capitol Hill. Those bigger changes will happen for sure during 2022 mid-term election and the year 2024 of the Presidential National Elections. With the GOP backing for former President Trump or some other top GOP faithful candidate be running as our next President. Will there be Glory Hallelujah Time again?

> Once you begin a great movement, there is no telling where it will end.
> We meant to change a nation, and instead we changed the world.
> President Ronald Reagan

The Bible tells us we need faithful leaders in our business world, also from the mayors all the way to the White House that they have knowledge, understanding, and wisdom with the Love of Jesus in their heart for a greater love for our America greatness. Let's pray that God again will have mercy for our country to rise up such men and women making our America greater again. Jesus is all we need for He is the only lasting loving hope for today and all those tomorrows yet to come. We must pray with authority for our country, our communities, and special our children and their children for they are the ones that will suffer the most. It's time to cry out, "O Lord Jesus Christ have mercy and hear our prayers, come into our life and give us that blessing hope, greater joy, more love in our hearts, and with greater peace of mind."

> Will you revive us again, that your people may
> rejoice in you?
> (Psalm 85:6)

> You are my servant, I have chosen you and
> have not reject you.
> So do not fear, for I am with you; do not be
> dismayed, for I am your God
> I will strengthen you and help you; I will
> upheld you with my rightness hand.
> (Isaiah 41:9-10)

> Call to me and I will answer you and tell you
> great and unsearchable things you may not
> know.
> (Jeremiah 33:3)

America is calling for God's helping hand with all the terrible health issues as COVID-19 or any coming pandemics; the unknown evil war-like leadership of Red China, North Korea, and Russia facing our America and rest the world. Also, the out of control Caravan invasion at the southern border, and the financial concerns for the hard working families be facing with higher inflation-taxation and recession fears for the year 2022 going into the next two years. The big real question How and will the far-left Forty-sixth President and his far-left socialism administration fixing all the bad conditions of our country which they had created in the first place?

At this time I will take you from those "Doom and Gloom" serious trouble conditions facing America by adding some lighter humor.

By having the Lady Vice President running up the golden brick road to see the Wizard of OZ to invited him or one of his much wisdom top advisors come to Capitol Hill by given their wildest answer and opinion from their crystal ball in order to fixed our country's with so many mess-ups. The very next day of his arrival, Mr. President, Lady Vice President, Lady Speaker of the House, and rest of the D Party administration was there with open arms with that ole fashion red carpet welcome. In come Professor XYZ Do Little, the President, College of Hard Knocks, a short bald headed man wearing a gray flannel suit of the late 1939's, having very thick eye glasses because one eye is far-sighed and other eye is near-sighted. With a brief case in one hand and a 3 legged stool in the other hand, he gave us that old silly looking grin. As he set on his 3 legged stool by reaching into his brief case for those items for his assignment, next put on his green eye shades and his sleeve garters. By saying "How goes the world today?" Most important of all by saying "Just maybe for sure your views of reality is distorted all the time, just obey the Ten Commandments and God Will Bless America?" Got up with his brief case in one hand and his 3 legged stool in the other hand, next went up to Secretary of the Treasury by saying "Here is my statement just pay me with a box of gold bricks from Fort Knox for my services." As he was leaving by saying, "For any more economic and financial advice just talk with my friends the Lion for greater courage, the Scarecrow for outstanding wisdom, and the Tin Man for that heart of love." As he leaving by saying "Going back to Kansas walking up the golden brick road to see the Wizard of OZ for my next crystal ball assignment."

IT TWO, GOD and YOU, we must pray for our America and their Leaders.

NINE

America Must Faithful Relation With Israel

The purpose of this chapter bring out the main reasons why the land of Israel and their people is important for America and rest the world. Israel was called by the Lord to be His Holy Nation from the first day and up to the last days. God always had a plan and purpose for His beloved land of Israel and mostly for His people that He so loved, for He has protected them for thousands of years. As it was in the days of old, there are those countries of this world even during this twenty-first century who seek to harm and even destroy Israel. Being the Good Shepherd, Jesus will protect His sheep with total safety and their security. The near years yet to come for the second coming as their Messiah, then they will believe for sure when they see Him Face to Face. Their Messiah, the King of kings and Lord of lords was there for them even on the cross. Our Lord Jesus with His saints, which are the born again, will put the final end to all this unrest for His beloved land of Israel and His people. In those last days it will become the War of all wars which only Israel will survive, all the evil nation be gone forever.

Israel is the birthplace of the Jewish people. It's here that the Jew's political, religious, and spiritual identity was established. After being forcibly exiled from their land for several years because they had forsaken the covenant of the Lord their God, those people kept and return to their faith and never ceased to pray for the restoration of political freedom. Israel signed their Declaration of Independence on May 14, 1948, the interim government of Israel took control. The first day of statehood for Israel was May 15, 1948 when the United Nations recognize Israel being reborn in one day as a nation. This was the day of Pentecost for His beloved land as their Messiah. God's timeclock is now complete with His plans and purpose for the rebirth of His beloved Israel. The 1967 Six Day War, Israel outstanding Air-force results of Operation Focus defected Egypt, Jordan, and Syria by destroying their airfields and air planes. After many hundreds years, God's people are now in their land never leave again. The Fig trees sprout their leaves for Israel. What a Blessing of all blessings and Promise of all promises.

America, always be with Israel as faithful partners all the time, whether it's good or hard times for their country and their people. This small country of the world is facing many uncertain times with those world's countries who are always against Israel and wanting to wipe that country of Israel off the world map. We must always have faithful leadership in Washington D.C. to keep this faithful relationship alive between our country and the land of Israel. America will protect Israel in this twenty-first century just like Queen Esther and Mordecai did for the Jews many hundreds years ago. Those two spoke up and stood their ground not given up for their faithful living by protecting those Jewish people, that Queen Esther and Mordecai loved so much.

IT TAKE TWO, GOD and YOU for America and Israel working together for greater Freedom and Liberty.

> I will make you into a great nation and I will bless you; and I will make your name great, and you will be a blessing.
> I will bless those who bless you, and whoever curses you, I will curse; and all the people on earth will be bless through you.
> (Genesis 12: 2-3)
>
> Israel will be saved by the Lord with everlasting salvation; you will never be put to shame or disgraced, to ages everlasting.
> (Isaiah 45:17)
>
> I will also make you a light for the Gentiles, that you may bring my salvation to the ends of the earth.
> (Isaiah 49:6)
>
> I will make them one nation in the land, on the mountain of Israel. There will be one king over them all and they shall no longer be two nations or be divided into two kingdoms.
> They will be my people, and I will be their God.
> (Ezekiel 37: 22-23)

It was glorious time for Israel when their people return to

the land of their first love. There they will seek and see the second coming of their Messiah. God have blessed them for thousands of years bring them with refreshed blossom joy and that living peace and now it is true for sure.

> I will be like the dew to Israel; he will blossom like a Lily. Like a cedar in Lebanon he will send down his shoots; his young roots will grow.
> His splendor will be like an olive tree, his fragrance like a cedar of Lebanon.
> Men will dwell again in the shade. He will flourish like the grain. He will blossom like a vine and his fame will be like the wine from Lebanon.
> (Hosea14: 5-7)

> I will plant Israel in their own land, never again to be uprooted from the land I have given them.
> (Amos9:15)

> May those who love you be secure.
> May there be peace within your walls and security within your citadels.
> For the sake of my brothers and friends, I will say, "Peace be with you. For the sake of the house of the Lord our God.
> (Psalm 122:6-8

Israel has many names as these: Emmanuel Land, God's Holy Land, Land of Milk and Honey, the Lord's Land, and the Promise Land, likewise Israel is the Apple of God's Eye. God is the center of the universe for Israel become the center of the world. God created the people of Israel to be God's servant and the country of Israel to be the total light to all nations. Because our Lord Jesus came to take away darkness of sins and bring total light of salvation to the whole wide world. Everything posed by the light becomes visible for it is the light that makes everything visible. Israel was not see itself as better than other nations, but as the only real tool with God's hands for the benefit of all nations. The people of Israel are God's chosen children for evermore.

In this new twenty-first century, Israel is one of the riches country in the world with great abundance of crops and fruits, being economy and financial sound, up to date medical sources, military strong, and they have abundance of water. Can you believe that at one time many years ago this small country was a big unknown land without anything of great value and now it a country with plenty. God has blessed His land and His people for it is now the lighthouse for all nations with its flashing outreaching light beams. His land will shine like the bright light of the sun and be the total light for the whole wide world for evermore. Thousands years ago God created the whole wide universe, even in this twenty-first century God still holds Israel as the center of the whole wide world for our Heavenly God will always be holding the whole wide world in His protective hands.

> When your heads and flocks grow large and
> your silver and your gold increase, and all that
> you have is multiplied; then your heart will
> become proud and you will forget the Lord

your God. You may say to yourself, "My power and the strength of my hands have produced the wealth for me."
But remember the Lord your God for it is he who gives you the ability to produce wealth, and to confirms his covenant, which he swore to your forefathers, as it is today.
(Deuteronomy8: 13, 17-18)

For the sake of the house of the Lord our God, I will see your prosperity.
(Psalm 122: 9)

Blessing and prosperity will be yours.
(Psalm 128:2)

There is no city like Jerusalem on the face of the earth. Jerusalem is the capital of His beloved land of Israel, it become the chosen city of God for His chosen people. We must be praying for Israel and the city of Jerusalem each day for they are God's first and only Love. That our America will always keep Israel in our loving care as the same way God kept His land in His loving care. This been true from the days of the old Promise Land of Milk and Honey and even up to the present twenty-first century. Forty-fifth President Donald J. Trump announced December 2017 that America would recognize Jerusalem as Israel's capital and moved the United States Embassy from Tel Aviv to Jerusalem. Thank goodness that this American President Trump with his Vice President Pence are faithful true friend to Israel and their people. The prior Forty-fourth President was unfaithful to the land of

Israel and their people. That is why our America was not bless by God for those years under his unfaithful leadership. Because of this unfaithful president, our America went thru the worst recession of the last seventy years. My dear Brothers and Sisters in Christ be careful and be sure who you vote for in any local, state, and mostly of those presidential national elections. We need and want both faithful president and vice president being faithful true friend and a good neighbor to the people of Israel. God said many thousand years ago that He bless any nation that will bless his Israel and their people. Bless and be Blessed.

> Pray for the peace of Jerusalem:
> May the prosper who love you.
> (Psalm 122: 6)

> For the Lord has chosen Zion, for he has desired it has his dwelling place:
> This is my resting place for ever and ever.
> (Psalm 132: 13-14)

> This is what the Sovereign God says:
> This is Jerusalem, I have set it in the center of the nations, with countries all around her.
> (Ezekiel 5:5)

Most of the Jews have returned to Israel from all the world to live in their own land and having Jerusalem as their undivided capital. At last they are in their Promise Land for God always love His land of milk and honey.

Blessed the nation whose God is the Lord the
people he chose for his inheritance.
(Psalm 33:12)

The good news is that the Holy City, the New Jerusalem,
created by God in heaven will be coming down in glory out
of the third heaven and be with the new heaven and the new
earth. This glorious Holy New Jerusalem will be our future
home for every faithful Christian believer, those born again,
for evermore. This beautiful huge Holy City of God will be
laid out some 1,400 cubits-miles foursquare. That is 1,400
miles high, 1,400 long, and 1,400 miles wide. There will be
lots of joyful times being with our Christian faithfully family
and friends. Most important we will be living and seeing
our Lord Jesus face to face and all the Saints from years ago.
Yes, we will have that special heavenly job to serve our Lord
Jesus. It will be Hallelujah time, be Praising time, and good
ole Gospel Singing time with our Lord Jesus, the Angeles,
and all the Saints.

Then I saw a new heaven and a new earth, or
the first heaven and the first earth had passed
away, and there was no longer any sea.
I saw the Holly City, the new Jerusalem,
coming down out of heaven from God,
prepared as a bride beautifully dressed for
her husband. And I heard a loud voice from
the throne saying "Now the dwelling of God
is with men, and he will live with them. They
will be his people, and God himself will be
with them and be their God. He will wipe

every tear from their eyes. There will be no more death or mourning or crying or pain, for the old order of things has passed away." (Revelation 21: 1-4)

He said to me: "It is done. I am the Alpha and the Omega, the Beginning and the End.
To him who is thirsty I will give to drink without cost from the spring of the water of life.
He who overcome will inherit all this, and I will be his God and be my son." (Revelation 21: 6-7)

Our America must always remember, that God only blessed those countries or nations that bless His Holly Land of Israel and His people, and curse those countries and nations that curse His Holly Land and His people. God has called on America to bless and protect His Promise Land and His people. This is an outstanding calling from our Heavenly Father for America to bless the most holy land of Israel and His people. This special calling is a Blessing of all blessing for America. The last twenty years of this twenty-first century, my question to you is, "Are you seeing your America blowing in the wind because of various government people have turned their backs on Israel?" We have seen this with those years under the so-call leadership of the Forty-fourth President. This unfaithful president turned his back several times on Israel with his many disagreements with the Prime Minister of Israel, Benjamin Netanyahu. This situation will happen again or even worst because the far-left D Party has won the 2020 Presidential National Election. When this new leadership in Washington turn toward socialism, our America will never be the same Christian country again. In that terrible situation our Heavenly Father may not have any mercy for America. Our America must never forsake God's Holy Land of Israel and their people. Otherwise, there will be God's judgment on this country or any other country that is not a friend of Israel. We must always have faithful leadership there on Capitol Hill of Washington in order keeping this faithful relationship alive and well between America and the land of Israel.

> May those who bless you blessed and those
> who curse you be cursed.
> (Numbers 24:9)

During those years under the unfaithful leadership of the Forty-fourth President and with the Fourth-sixth President is one of the main reasons why our America went backward being a financial and military world power leader. We must always work faithful and honest together for that better relationship between our America and God's Holy Land of Israel for that extra blessings from our Heavenly Father. America is thankful having great men like both President Donald J. Trump and Vice President Mike Pence being our faithful outstanding leaders for our beloved country. They are strong faithful-minded men and great friends of Israel, their people, and with the Prime Minister. As always our Heavenly Father with His Son, our Lord Jesus, will watch over their Israel like a Good Shepherd watches over his sheep. You are my people for I'm your God.

The Lord is my shepherd, I shall not be in want.
(Psalm 23:1)

Unless and until our America will turn back the faithful ways of "In God We Trust" our country will be just like the children of Israel many hundreds years ago. Godlessness has shown us what happens when we don't trust God. America has turned its back on God over the years, thankful we have a forgiven Heavenly Father for He will not turn his back on his faithful children of America. Our America has been warned by God just like He did when His people entered the 'Promise Land" many thousand years ago.

Six million Jews were perished in the Holocaust. They were the ones got off those over-crowed train cars enter into German concentration camps like Auschwitz, the young and strong people went to the work camps while the old and weak ones for that certain death. Today, many who survived lived in poverty, they are the one that escape death many years ago only to be left with no one to care for them late in life. We are thankful for the financial support and the helping people thru the organization of the International Fellowship of Christians and Jews with God Blessings.

Is it not to share your food with the hungry and to provide the poor with shelter when you see the naked, to clothe him, and not turn away fr0m your own flesh and blood?
(Isaiah 58: 7)

Let them give thanks to the Lord for his unfailing love and his wonderful deeds for

men, for he satisfied the thirsty and fills the hungry with good things.
(Psalm 107: 8-9)

For I was hungry and you gave me something to eat, I was thirsty and you gave me something to drink, I was a stranger and you invited me in, I need clothes and you clothed me, I was sick and looked after me.
(Matthew 26: 35-36)

Let God's Promise Shine on your Problems.
Corrie ten Boom

God has lay on my heart to pray for His beloved Israel and the love for His People, please join me in prayer.

Oh Lord, watch over your Israel, its Holy city of Jerusalem, and your people, as a Good Shephard that watch over His sheep in those green pastures beside that quite waters for their safety and security. You are the Savior for their Salvation and for being the wonderful Messiah by seeing Him face to face.
Thank you Oh Lord, for all your blessing and love by taken your people from those valleys of hopeless to the very mountain top of forever blessings, that living hope, and love with greater peace.
Will pray this in your name. Amen.

As the mountains surrounded Jerusalem, so the Lord surrounds his people both now and forever.
(Psalm 125: 2)

IT TAKES TWO, GOD and YOU for America always be faithful friend with Israel.

TEN

Having Bible and Going To Church

My dear faithful Christian Brothers and Sisters in Christ, your children, and grandchildren, I will bring you the following information in the next two chapters by helping you find a church for your family, your friends, and mostly any unsaved person. Also, some background history of both Christian radio and Christian TV stations. They are the ones bring the good news of our Lord Jesus each day and night.

Our Lord has giving our America so many churches in our home towns across America, that we can go to any church, denomination, or any none-denomination church of our choice. We are most thankful to be able have a Bible in our homes even while traveling, there Bibles in motels or hotels. Whatever your denomination, there is a church for you and your family that will fulfill your spiritual needs. There are some evil countries of this world where it is unlawful have a Bible or being a Christian. Recall during those terrible times of World War11 where German solders with orders from the evil top leadership killing all those Jews for their faith. It was alive on Fox TV news the year 2020 where few faithful men on their knees in the process of beheaded. God has a special place in hell for that kind evil leadership. Don't have any government or some organization take away your religious freedom, you speak up and stand up for your Christian believes. What is most important that you will find a Bible-preaching and Bible-teaching church or denomination church that believes in the love of Jesus with the Word of God in all the 1,189 chapters or 31,100 Bible verses from the books from Genesis to the book of Revelation. There are so many denomination churches that don't preached and teach regarding the near coming of the Rapture and that of the end times or the last days during this church age. This must change for the main reason the Holy Book is 25 percent Bible prophecy. Parents with children, Sunday school and summer vacation bible school is a must for teaching the young ones the Word of God with the Love of Jesus Christ. The future of the church is in the hands of the little children. They will become the Christian leaders and faithful people for tomorrow's generation. Our Heavenly Father's plans and purpose for the people of this world, that these people thru their faith with the grace and love of Jesus, as our Savior, be born again for their forever salvation.

The church, the family, the home, and faithful good teachers are where good goals and values are formed for your children and their children. As believing faithful parents take extra time of togetherness for daily reading and studying Bible, togetherness for daily prayer, togetherness going to church each week, and togetherness for those family playful times. With these in mind as faithful parents will be creating a greater future for your children and greater future for our America. Where there a church you will find fellowship and love, where there is fellowship and love you will find believers. Where there are believers in a church you will find God, where there is God you will find our Lord Jesus, where there Jesus you find salvation thru your faith and Word of God.

You have the right having a Bible in your home and going to your church, this is according to those faithful words of the Declaration of Independence and the first Amendment of the America's Constitution, this is called freedom of religion. There are federal government people on Capitol Hill in Washington D.C. wanting to change our conservative Constitution and the Ten Amendments. This must never happen for this is our freedom and religion rights. The following words is regarding the first Amendment of the Constitution of the United States of America:

> Congress shall make no law respecting an
> establishment of religion, or prohibiting the
> free exercise thereof; or abridging the freedom
> of speech, or of the press, or the right of the
> people peaceable to assemble, and to petition
> the Government for a redress of grievances.

By radio and TV, we can hear and watch any Christian program of our choice. Don't let the courts or any anti-Christian groups take away Christian radio and Christian TV programs off the air. Be aware of the unfaithful organizations such as the American Civil Liberties Union, better known as ACLU. For many years, they've been one of the greatest threats to our freedom of religion by taking away God's Holy Word and prayer from all faithful Christians, your church, and mostly our country. If this happen there be no freedom of the press, freedom of religion, and freedom of speech. My Christian Friends lets become more believing faithful Brothers and Sisters in the name of Jesus Christ, let's stand firm and tall for our America rights for it's your duty and your rights because of these three freedoms.

Those radio and TV minsters are always preaching God's Word with the love of Jesus Christ for your salvation. These are the end times for this church age, always be looking up, always be ready, and always be watching for His coming in the sky for His Church which will be the Rapture. We must put our trust in our God each day during these difficult times. Financial support is always needed for both Christian radio and TV stations to stay on the air. Please do your share with your church as their greater mission for this great out reach all in God's glory and for His Son, our Lord Jesus Christ.

IT TAKES TWO, GOD and YOU to keep the Good News on the airways.

When I travel by car or relaxing in my home, I always enjoy hearing the Good News on Christian radio stations. My favorite local radio station is King of Kings Radio Network founded the year 1987 by the founder and president Rev. Dr. David Carr. Under his faithful leadership at the main headquarters location in Somerset, Kentucky which now has ten radio stations reaching out to different states. They keep adding more stations when they can all in the Glory for our Heavenly Father. The Gospel of our Lord Jesus is being reaching out in faith with God's glory into the following eight states: Illinois, Indiana, Kentucky, Missouri, Ohio, Tennessee, Virginia, and West Virginia. What a wonderful God's Blessing for this greater outreach being done all for His glory. WWOG 90.9 FM out of my hometown Cookeville, Tennessee is one of those radio stations. These radio stations just like that of WWOG provides gospel music and preaching around the clock every day of the year. From this radio station, I enjoy hearing Cross Talk and those true stores by life people of the program known as "Unshackle" put on by Pacific Garden Mission out of Chicago. "Unshackle" has been on the radio since 1950, it's the longest radio program on the air. By having true-life stories regarding those people going through some hard time in their lives with problems of drinking liquor, being hook and selling drugs, gambling, and stealing, which in turn caused marriage break ups, loss of jobs, and being depressed by turning into homeless. Later those homeless people hearing the Good News of Jesus Christ at some church or at a rescue mission. They turn to God for their salvation, it became the blessing hope for their lives. It will bless you by hearing those great stories of how God change those homeless or the needy people into faithful greater lives. Some of those born again people went to some Bible college and later became ministers by serving their Lord. Our God is in total control of the Gospel airways let's be keeping this Gospel alive.

Pacific Garden Mission is a Christian organization founded the year 1877 in Chicago by George and Sarah Clark. It might be the largest and for sure one of the oldest America's rescue mission. They providing free clothing, three meals each day, housing for men, and separate housing for women with children. There are dentist and medical doctors providing free medical care for those in need. The good news there are trained counselors helping with personal needs and pastors and ministers providing church services and other faithful religious needs. This outstanding rescue mission is always there helping those needy people or the homeless back on the recovery road in their lives and most important for their own salvation being heaven bound. This old "lighthouse" rescue mission providing the blessed hope for a better future to those homeless, needy, and the unsaved people. Everyone are welcome for the alive radio program of Unshackle just come as you are.

IT TAKES TWO, GOD and YOU, bless this old lighthouse as it blessed many people.

This is true story of a man name Richard with a life seem be uncontrollable with the drug habit for several years. His life was living on the streets and being in jail or prison more than ten years. One day being sleeping on a dirty mattress in a basement the summer of 2011, reality hit him and he begin to think about a new and different life for himself. Richard's days began filled with thoughts of some way to get back on his feet. His problem was finding someone who give him another chance. He came to the Cookeville, Tennessee Rescue Mission. Stating "No one that know my history did not want see him anymore, not even my own parents." There at that rescue mission he found people that cared. He received free clothing, food, and shelter. Most important of all he needed spiritual help and received it. He began to explore his spiritual life, by study the Bible and going to church at this Mission. For the last several years he is now saved, baptized, and working at the Mission. The good news is that he went from the streets to become an honor student. He graduated with Bachelor of Arts degree in 2018 at Tennessee Tech University here in Cookeville and have plans return to his hometown to work. He had stated "I know now that God was always there waiting and watching for me to make my decision and finally I did. I thank God for giving me that one more opportunity and I tell him so every day." What a nice story to share what God can do thru a rescue mission for anyone, even for a person like Richard. Our Heavenly Father is always there all the time for all your needs by just asking with a prayer anytime and receive those wonderful blessings.

Bless this Cookeville Rescue Mission and so many other missions like Pacific Gardens with your financial gifts or your gifted talents are always helpful and thankful.

IT TAKES TWO, GOD and YOU, blessing comes with those financial support and helping hands to your local rescue mission.

ELEVEN

Preaching By Radio And TV

Our gospel preaching has come a long way. Years ago, it was the very faithful missionary people with their ham radios going into the jungles and the wilds of the world. Next came men of God known as the Circular Riders preaching by horseback riding from community to villages. Around the mid-turn of the twenty century or even before, the Gospel being preached by faithful men in tent revivals like those of Dwight L. Moody, William "Billy" Sunday, Billy Graham, Oral Roberts, and many others for they were spreading the Good News of our Lord Jesus. About thirty-five years ago, there was a tent revival in my home town of Cookeville, Tennessee. This was a new experience for me being there for that great ole time revival.

The following words make a great revival. Rev. Dwight L. Moody once said, "I look upon the world as a vessel its ruin is nearer and nearer." God said to Moody, "Here is a lifeboat and rescue as many as you can before the ship sinks." When he preached it was like a voice speaking out with backing of the Holy Spirit. After more than 120 years from the time of

Moody preaching years, (he died in 1899), the end times or the last days are very much closer. There in Chicago people can go to the Moody Bible Institute in order to study for the ministry. What a Blessing of all blessings from this man of God with the outreach of the Gospel and it all started with God and one man. Each Sunday morning on the way to my church, I can hear by radio the Gospel being preached by senior pastor Dr. Erwin W. Lutzer from the Moody Church.

Shortly after being saved through the outreach of the Pacific Garden Mission in Chicago, William "Billy" Sunday gave up his professional baseball career to work full time for his and our Lord Jesus Christ. Rev. Billy Sunday (1862-1955) became the best-known and most influential American evangelist during the first two decades of the twenty century. Rev. Billy Sunday is still remembered today for his energetic preaching style much like a roaring whirlwind with large successful evangelistic campaigns across America. In his lifetime, he preached to over several million people in the days before loudspeaker, radios, and television. These are the words from Preacher Billy Sunday: "I am an old- fashion preacher of the old time religion, that has warmed this cold world for two thousand years."

Billy Graham start preaching in the late 1940's, the first one was held at Los Angeles. They were the old-fashion tent revivals. During that first revival there were 6,000 converts of his 350,000 listeners, he became the new evangelist arises by God. From that first revival to the next seventy years with his many crusades around the world his words from God were these: "Come to God, He will come in and transform your life. According to the authority of God's Word, you will know for sure of going to heaven."

Billy Graham's first radio broadcast was the "Hour of Decision" in 1950. It was in 1953 and from there on all Billy Graham's Crusades were fully integrated. As he preached these words: "Christianity is not a white man's religion and don't let anybody ever tell you it's white or black for Christ belongs to all people. He belongs to the whole world." Then in 1957 life on TV, history was made at his NYC Crusade which was held at Madison Square Garden. At one of those many NYC Crusades services, he had Dr. Rev. Martin Luther King Jr. to give the opening prayer for we are God's children. Because of this one crusade, it became the very start that God and our Lord Jesus belong to all the people. Billy Graham was the giver of God's Good News with the Word of God because of these following Bible verses:

> Go into the world and peach the good news to all creation. Whoever believes and is baptized will be saved, but whoever does not believe will be condemned.
> (Mark 16:15-16)

> The necessity of repenting from sin and turning to God, having faith in our Lord Jesus.
> (Acts 20:21)

> "Behold I am coming soon! I Jesus, have sent my angels to give you this testimony for the churches. I am the Root and Offspring David and the Morning Star.
> (Revelation 22:16)

We must be returning to God, having faith in our Lord Jesus.
We can be certain that God will give us the strength and resources we need to live through any situation in life that He ordains.
Billy Graham

God's calling this man out of North Carolina western mountains to become Pastor for God to preached in crusades of some 200 countries with an estimated total gathering between 200 and 250 million people. Billy Graham preached by faith: "Commit your life to Christ, for God's Promise is true." As the choir sing "Just as I Am," people by the thousand came forward for their salvation during each crusades. Now Franklin Graham, son of Billy Graham, has taken charge of the Billy Graham Evangelistic Association by preaching thru out America and around the world just like his father. Billy Graham's grandson, Will Graham, is preaching the Gospel around the world, this is the third generation of preachers in that one faithful family. His Decision America Tour 2016, Franklin Graham was leading prayer rallies and preaching in the Capitol cities of all fifty states. He believed the only hope from those nationwide revival, he said "We must preach the Gospel like never before." My own personal opinion because of this tour, that the 2016 National Presidential Election was won by the America's Forty-fifth President Donald J. Trump by taken the GOP all the way in Victory. September 2020 Franklin Graham held his Prayer March in the Nation Capitol for greater faithful America.

Dr. Rev. Billy Graham (1918-2018) the America's Pastor went to his heavenly home at the age of 99. The following words by the America Pastor:

"I have found that when I present the simple message the Gospel of Jesus Christ, with authority, quoting from the very Word of God. He takes that message and drives its supernaturally into the human heart." At those whole wide world crusades George Beverly Shea always be singing that ole gospel song "Just as I Am." That crusade song was written by Charlotte Elliott:

"Just as I Am"

> Just as I am, without one plea, but that Thy
> blood was shed for me.
> And that Thou bidd'st me come to Thee, O
> Lamb of God, I come I come!
>
> You become a model to all the believers.
> The Lord's message rang out from you for your
> faith in God has become known everywhere.
> (1 Thessalonian 1: 7-8)
>
> Pray that the Gospel will transform the hearts
> and lives of many who are searching for hope.
> Billy Graham

After reading the third Epistle of John: Beloved, I pray that you may prosper in all things and be in good health, just as your soul prosper. Rev. Oral Roberts started the year 1947 with his ministry of healing, salvation, and the delivering power of God as he conducted his ministry through faith healing crusades across the USA and around the world. Through those years he conducted more than 300 crusades on six continents and laid hands on two million people thru God's healing power. He was a pioneer in both radio and TV ministry that of the Abundant Life television revivals. Also, he is the founder of the outstanding Oral Roberts University for Christian education of Tulsa, Oklahoma. Before Rev. Oral Roberts went to heaven, he gave his son, Richard Roberts, that double portion anointing and blessing for the ministry to preach God's healing power of many health needs. It is like the old Bible story when Elijah the prophet given Elisha, also a prophet, a double portion of his blessing and spirit before he went to heaven in a chariot and horses of fire by going up like a roaring whirlwind.

Rev. Richard Roberts and his wife Lindsay have this TV ministry known as The Place of Miracles. God told him in a vision there be greater religious times ahead and it will become the time for: "It's greater Healing Time, it's greater Miracle Time, and greater Revival Time for America" what a blessing that it will be. During this new twenty-first century, God has a new healing ministry for Rev. Richard Roberts. God wants him become minister to pastors and church leaders, teach them the three principles of the healing power of God, the power of the Holy Spirit, and the power for sowing and reaping for people's health needs. Also, God want him to preach a stronger healing message on TV, plus continuing his school for healing on the internet. In order the Word of God and the Healing Power be going out to the whole wide world. With the powerful ministry of our Lord Jesus, this means the end-times and the last days of His Church is much closer. Which is a bigger sign that our Lord Jesus is coming soon for the Rapture. The Bible tell us to take the Gospel to the ends of the earth and sharing the Good News of healing and salvation for all the people.

> Jesus was born to step into a world of trouble and bring healing and deliverance, and that is the call of God upon my life to reach out to people in their troubles and heartaches, to pray and believe God, and to bring them His Word of hope and healing.
> Richard Roberts

The early TV ministry of this country were the founders of Christian Broadcasting, such as the following: Rev. Pat Robertson, Dr. Lester Sumrall, and Rev. Paul and Jan Crouch. The good news with TV Christian ministry, that we can have the Gospel being preach around the world farther and faster. With the Gospel of Jesus being preached, more people around the world will start believing the Word of God with the Love of Jesus.

Sixty years ago 1961-2021, Rev. Pat Robertson with his wife and family with just seventy dollars took a big step in faith started the first Christian TV station in America and build it into Christian Broadcasting Network (CBN), which is now located in Virginia Beach. He was the host of Christian program the 700 Club and the founder and president of Regent University located in the same city of CBN. God told him "Be about your work of bring the Gospel to the nations. I want heaven filled with people who believe in My Son." It was his faith to: "Command from the Lord to claim the airways from the Prince of Power of the air and give him the

Prince of Peace." His leadership with his son, Rev Gordon Robertson, for Operation Blessing has been outstanding, this Christian organization providing food, medical care, water, and various supplies to the needy throughout the world. After sixty faithful years Rev. Pat Robertson is now retired from CBN. As of February 2022 Rev. Gordon Robertson is now the new president for this outstanding Christian TV ministry. I have been financial supporting CBN with the 700 Club since the 1960s, let's be working together for this Christian outreached with the glory for our Heavenly Father and His Son, our Lord Jesus Christ.

In the early 1960, Dr. Lester Sumrall known as the "The Father of Christian TV," founded the Le SEA Broadcasting Network which is located near Indianapolis, Indiana. It is a multimedia network covering the globe to reach untold millions of people with the Good News of our Lord Jesus Christ. His vision is to "plow deep and wide" with the word of God and win million souls for our Lord Jesus. Dr. Sumrall has a good blessing saying: "Feed your faith and starve your doubts." His sons are now in charge of this outstanding TV ministry after their father passing away few years ago. What a blessing it was watching his TV ministry during those Indiana years.

Several years ago, I went to his TV station, Le Sea Broadcasting Network for a Full Gospel Businessmen meeting. It was there that I was born again or being saved and being filled with the Holy Spirit, next receiving the gift of that prayer spiritual language to my Heavenly Father. What a bigger change in my life with those wonderful blessings came from Him, it became wonderful time for Hallelujah Time and Praising Time. Those were outstanding blessing and faithful Hoosiers years being togetherness as a family for church and watching Christian TV with those faithful blessings.

Each night before going to bed, I get on my knees in prayer with that spiritual talking to my Heavenly Father and next pray in my English language. The good news by praying with faith in Jesus name for those purpose needs, He will answer with greater positive results to those prayers. Lord Jesus said "asked in faith and you will receive." Praised my Savior each day for my America, my born again faithful family and friends, my church family, those brave military and veterans.

In 1973 Rev. Paul and Jan Crouch co-founded the Trinity Broadcasting Networks (TBN), which is located in Costa Mesa, California and the Trinity Music City near Nashville. Under their leadership, TBN has grown become one of our country largest Christian TV networks. Both Paul and Jan Crouch are with their Lord in Heaven. Their son Rev. Matt Crouch and his wife Laurie are the host and ministers of TBN. With their leadership they will take this TV Ministry going forward until Jesus comes for His Church. God is in control of the airways for Christian TV to reach out to the whole wide world with His Holly Words.

It's because of the faithful leadership of these four people, there family, the working staff, and through their Christian Broadcasting TV stations with the satellites in the heavenly sky, that the people of this world are hearing the Good News and seeing it come more alive for your new faith of healing and salvation. It took faith and lots of prayers in the startup costs in those early months and years. God was there all the time and even now to answer those supporting prayers from those faithful financial partners. The first earth station satellites for seeing Christian TV ministry was in operation 1977 for the world to receive the Gospel of our Lord Jesus Christ. We have more advanced and better means thru the internet and smart phones by taken the Gospel farther and faster where it's most needed. Thankful for those faithful people with their gifted talents by creating such new devices for that greater reaching out to the world with the Living Word. Our Heavenly Father want everyone in every country and nations hear the Good News about His Son, our Lord Jesus Christ. By having more people being born again before the coming Rapture, for He does not want anyone be left behind.

That time is now in this twenty-first century for we have seen all the signs being fulfilled for that near coming of the Rapture which will be end of the Church Age. It looks like our Heavenly Father has put his arms around the world bring the Gospel to all the people. For sure our Lord Jesus is coming soon for His Church of the Rapture.

> Yes, I am coming soon. Come, Lord Jesus.
> The grace of the Lord Jesus be with God's
> people.
> (Revelation 22: 21-22)

We are hearing and seeing outstanding Christian men and women preaching the word of God on Christian TV stations every day and night never stopping. Some of my favorite Christian TV ministers are the following: Irvin Baxter-End of the Age, Dr. Rodney Howard Browne-The Great Awakening, Billy Graham with his many Crusades,

Rev. John Hagee of Cornerstone Church, Dr. Robert Jeffress of Pathway to Victory, Dr. David Jeremiah-Turning Point, Hal Lindsay-The Rapture, Rev. Robert Morris of Southlake Church, Rev. Richard Roberts-Place for Miracles, Rev. Pat Robertson- CBN of 700 Club, Rev. Perry Stone-Manna-Fest and so many other people of God sharing the Good News of Jesus Christ. With our Heavenly Father's calling these men of God for this outreaching Gospel with his Son, our Lord Jesus, all this is possible. Let's be Praising the Lord each day, every day.

It takes faithful men and women become pastors to be on fire with the Holy Spirit to reach out to the world the Word of God and with the Love of Jesus. So preach and teach with all your heart about the healing power and salvation for the people during these end times or last days before our Lord Jesus comes for His Church. Just keep on sharing the Gospel of the Living Word that God is True and Jesus is Love. These people of God will win many souls for the Kingdom of Heaven. We must cry out to God for another Great Awakening for these men and women of God that the Holy Spirit will moved across our country and rest the whole wide world. With those positive powerful purpose prayers as a wake-up call, we will have that breakthrough for that ole fashion revival time. We want the church be Alive with Victory for our Lord Jesus Christ. Keep looking up, be ready, and watch for Jesus be coming soon for His Church. With faith and doing the sinner prayer to Lord Jesus Christ, He will forgive your sins and provide your salvation to become heaven bound. As children of God with our gifted talents we will carry His cross for that out reaching Gospel.

It's the ministry faithfulness of those missionary people and those circuit riders to the modern age of radio and TV ministry that we are hearing and seeing the gospel being preached. Over seventy-five years ago, this was impossible to preach the gospel around the world. With the modern age of TV with the satellites in the heavens it's like seeing our Lord Jesus putting His arms around the world with the Gospel for the glory of the Heavenly Father. As technology has progressed with advancement things as the internet and smartphones, we are seeing more ways of spreading the Gospel farther, faster, and smarter around the world. These are major impact today for preaching the Gospel more than any time in our world history.

Every day, God's people are reaching out the lost and the hurting with the message of hope. This greater hope movement is like those of the World Gospel Mission of Marion, Indiana providing financial support for the missionary. Also, the St. Labre Indian School of Ashland, Montana with Father Curtis's leadership providing outstanding Christian education-schooling for the Crow and Northern Cheyenne Indians. Those students with their outstanding Christian background, Christian education, and working experience will provide a better future for their own people. When the world appears to be darker each passing day, we cling the knowledge that light of Jesus will shines into the darkness for the likes of WGM and St. Labre School by keeping Christ's light into the world for that greater hope.

It takes great deal of money spreading the Gospel for Missions and both Christian radio and Christian TV stations during these end times or last days of this church age. Have your church in this financial goal as part of their outreach

Gospel mission. Many blessing with love from our God to you and your church.

The end-time signs being seen in the twentieth century and now more than ever in this twenty-first century. If you don't believe it, just read your daily newspaper headlines or see the night-time TV news of what is really happening in our America and rest of the world. For the real facts just start with your daily Bible study time for the Word of God what is happening today and the future telling us that these are the end times and that our Lord Jesus is coming back soon for His Church. In the last several years, I can feel it, I can hear it, and I can see it that our Lord Jesus is coming very soon in the big sky for His Church.

The very last sign of the end times or the last days of this church age is the Gospel be preached to all nations. That last Gospel preaching-teaching sign is happening today. Recalled going a trip few years ago with my wife to Scotland for the purpose seeing where our family roots came from. That Sunday morning in our hotel room, I turned on the TV to hear and see a local church service. To our surprise what we saw, it was The Hour of Power from the Glass Cathedral with Rev. Robert Schuler all the way from California. This Gospel being preach across America, then across the Atlantic Ocean, and finally into a hotel room in Scotland.

Praise the Lord, Jesus is coming soon. Always Keep looking up, always being Keep ready, and always Keep watching to hear God's calling for the Rapture of His Church. The Lord Jesus Christ will be coming from the Heaven of all heavens with a loud command by the Lord himself, with the voice of the archangel, and the trumpet call of God for taken all the born again Christians heavenly home. This is only possible by your faith and the grace and the love thru our Lord Jesus that all born again Christians be going home with Him. Because Jesus loves everyone, lets love Him even more by carrying the cross of healing and salvation with greater love for our Lord Jesus.

> A new command I give you: Love one another.
> As I love you, so you must love one another.
> By this all men will know that you are my disciples,
> If you love one another.
> (John 13:34-35)

Our churches across this country need more faithful Bible preaching to uplift people's spirits. I have heard there is a shortage of people going into the ministry. Lot of cases it took one or two years to find pastor, minister, and priest after one leaves or retires. This must change for the sake of our young generation and the future generation yet to come. According to the Billy Graham Evangelic Association that 1,500 pastors are leaving the ministry each month. The good news is that at the Billy Graham Training Center at the Cove near Asheville, North Carolina are providing the Pastors Renewal Project Program. This is an outstanding opportunity for pastors to be rejuvenated for their continuing work for the Kingdom of God. The Tennessee Bible College in my home town are providing training programs for ministers to stay in the work for our Lord Jesus. According to most recent survey that 50 percent of pastors make less than fifty thousand dollars per year. Also, 60 percent of pastors do not have health insurance and retirement package for their retirement golden years.

Church members this must change by keeping the gospel alive. Church attendance began to change in the 1960's and the trend has not reverse in this twenty-first century with percentage on the decline.

Christian radio station WWOG 90.9 FM of Cookeville, Tennessee survey dated November 2021, that church attendance has dropped to 45 percent. About 70 percent of people go church only on Easter and Christmas services. Going to church is not important to many Americans as was years ago. Some denominations have seen their membership shrink almost in half since the 1960's. The younger generation known as the Millennials are attending church less than their parents and their grandparents. Smaller churches in various communities and villages with twenty-five people or less in attendance are facing difficult financial times keeping their doors open. There are cases where some ministers have two or three small churches for weekly Sunday services or monthly services. Is this "the falling away of the church" as stated in the Bible? The Church is alarmed, but they must stay the course. Christians and church pastors must hold-on to the truth, faithfully proclaim, and live it. I recall several years ago, it was "The Blue Laws" that most of the eating places and stores for shopping were closed every Sunday morning in order people can attend church services. Now most these business places are opened every day except Christmas. Week-end shopping or sports events maybe the reason for people not going to church, or they are too busy in this fast pace world.

Just look around your church most of the members are older people. It is true at my church in my home town of Cookeville. We are concern that the next generation of followers won't follow through. Our Lord always will come to the rescued with faithful leaders and members to lead again as our Heavenly Father with the backing of the Holy Spirit preparing the way for His Church. It is a real blessing in my heart seeing young married couples come to church with their baby and children. Jesus Christ is head of His Church the same yesterday, today, and evermore. During these end times or the last days of the church age, we need to encourage each other so people should not fight or fused over denomination and doctrines difference. When we are born again or being saved, we become God's Christian Children as part of His Church in the coming rapture. This was possible with our faith and thru the grace and love of our Lord Jesus Christ being the Savior for our salvation.

All church pastors be aware what is happening across our America, regarding the gay movement that are making major changes to various denomination, maybe your church. The years 2021 into2024 and those years yet to come as many denomination churches like the Catholic and the United Methodist are facing many unknown conditions being split-apart as members going their separate ways. This regarding forming same-sex marriage by their church pastor with some member's approval. The big question facing the church is this right or wrong having same-sex marriage at any church or those church denomination? Will the time come in the near future having so call "gay person" become the church pastor? What the future holds for other denomination churches and from the strong minded Christian's viewpoints, only time will tell?

What coming next? The Bible tell us do not love the ways of the world, but stay with the holy ways and the Word of our

Heavenly Father and His Son, our Lord Jesus Christ. The ways of God last forever, but the ways of the world will pass away forever.

> Do not love the world or anything in the world. If anyone loves the world, the love of the Father is not in him. For everything in the world- the cravings of sinful man, the lust of his eyes and boasting of what he has and does- comes not from the Father but from the world. The world and its desires pass away, but the man who does the will of God lives forever. (1 John 2: 15-17)

With our daily faithfulness with God's Word, we will find strength for today and brighter hope for tomorrow. God wants His Church be one that is Alive, one build on Solid Rock of the Word of God, and one in Victory of total love for our Lord Jesus. We want Victory in Jesus every day of our lives. We must keep the Gospel alive up to the time of His coming for His Church. When the church with those faithful people are building and working together, they are creating stronger outreaching Gospel for their church and for our Lord Jesus Christ. God wants the church build on the Solid Rock with good strong cornerstones and foundation.

Few miles where I was born is this small white-frame church, the New Maysville Community Church, the last twenty-five years when I made trips back to Indiana always when to that church. The late Preacher Frank Bunn would have a powerful Lord's message, no white-wash sermons from this preacher-man for he told it like it is. He would always end his sermons by saying "Keep looking up." Let's be looking up for the near coming Rapture. If your church is any size of being small or large in attendance each Sunday services. Come lets us sing together this ole time religious song:

"The Little Church in the Wildwood"

> There's a church in the valley by the wildwood
> no lovelier ever spot in the dale;
> no place is so dear to my childhood, as the little church in the vale.
> How sweet on a clear Sunday morning, to list to the clearing bell; its tones so sweetly are calling, Oh, come to the church in the vale,
> If you do not stand firm in your faith, you will not stand.
> (Isaiah 7:9)

> Do not be afraid little flock, for your Father has been please to give you the Kingdom.
> (Luke 12:32)

The goal of the church is to spread God's living word throughout the world. Next, the church wants each person be born again for their salvation, so they be more than ready for the near coming Rapture and being heaven bound. If desired each person being baptized in the Holy Spirit of our Lord Jesus. However, being baptized is not required of going to heaven.

The following words is to state some of the purpose for of the Church:

- The Church is the calling to reach out for the love of Jesus Christ with the word of God.
- The Church is the body of Christ for He is the head of the church.
- The Church is the family of God.
- The Church is the bride of Christ.
- The Church is for being born again or saved for our salvation.
- The Church main and primary purpose is to worship God and His Son Jesus Christ.

It cannot be done without faith, hope, and love for these came from our Heavenly Father.

> Love is patient, love is kind. It does not envy, it does not boast, it is not self-proud. It is not easily angered it keeps no record of wrongs. Love does not delight in evil but rejoices with the truth. It always protects, always trusts, always hopes, always perseveres. Love never fails.
> (1 Corinthians 13: 4-8)

> And now these three remain: faith, hope, love, but the greatest of these is love.
> (1 Corinthians 13: 13)

Some words of wisdom from the Bible when a Pharisees asked the following question to our Lord Jesus:

> Teacher, which is the greatest commandment of the Law? Jesus replied: "Love the Lord your

God with all your heart and with all our soul
and with all your mind. This is the first and
greatest commandment. And the second is
like it:
Love your neighbor as yourself.
(Matthew 22: 36-39)

We are living in prophetic uncertain times as our Jesus
Christ will be returning from the heavenly sky for His
Church. Our Lord Jesus Christ is The KINGS of kings,
The LORD of lords, and the PRINCE of peace. He wants
His Church always be glorious, victorious, and a winning
one. Also, our Lord wants the same for our America that is
glorious, victorious, and winning.

IT TAKES TWO, GOD YOU with the Church by keeping
Gospel Alive on radio and TV.

TWELVE

The Coming Rapture

The people of our America and those around the world are hungry for God's Soul Food, His Word, and thirsty for God's Living Water. It's time for all the Churches get on their knees in prayer, because our country is in need for a coast to coast revival. During these end-times or last days of this church age, let's be getting more people born again or saved before His coming in the heavenly big sky or it will too late for the unsaved. Always working for His Church until the good Lord comes for you and for His Church which will be soon. Our Lord Jesus wants His Church be alive and His Church be preaching and teaching the gospel with Faith in victory. Preach with your heart just like that old song written by John H. Yates:

"Faith in the Victory"

Faith in the victory! Faith in the victory!
Oh, glorious victory That overcomes the world.

Spiritual sleeping churches across America are not preaching about Bible prophecy regarding the end times or last days, the Rapture, and the books of Daniel, Isaiah, Zechariah, and mostly Revelation. In those churches how many people will be looking up, be ready to go, and be watching? Maybe some of those people in those churches might miss the Rapture. Will God and His Son, our Lord Jesus, be happy and please with that church, that church denomination, and their pastors with those white-wash preaching? One preacher told me few years ago they did not teach about those end times in the Bible College where he went. All Bible Colleges should be reviewing what they are teaching and making fast and more necessary real changes. Because 25 percent of the Bible is prophecy. These are the prophecy words from our Heavenly Father which are most Holy, the most real, and the most truthful within the Holy Bible from Genesis to Revelation. This is the big reason to be preaching and teaching Bible prophecy. Since we are this close to the Rapture, all unsaved people should be running to the church alter. Our Lord Jesus will be there at any church with open arms with open caring heart for anyone. Our Lord will be saying these kind words "You are my Son and my Daughter, I am your Shepard and your Savior. Come as you are to the House of God for the doors are always open. My alter is there for everyone, every time, and everywhere." Our Jesus will be there for your salvation and restore your soul. After the Rapture, you will be going to your heavenly home, the Heaven of all heavens. Always stay close with Jesus wherever God and as the Holy Spirit leads you, with no turning back. Follow Jesus whatever, wherever, and whoever with no turning back.

Ask and it will be given to you; seek and you find; knock and the door will be opened to you. For every one who asks receives; he who seeks will finds; and to him who knocks, the door will be open.

How much will your heavenly Father give good gifts to those ask him.

(Matthew 7: 7-8,11)

Churches of this twenty-first century must always keep their doors open for those who are asking, seeking, and knocking. I believe that our Lord Jesus wants us Christians be better informed of what is happened in the many parts of the world, mostly our own America. We must be reading and study the Bible each day. It tells the future of the church, our country, our lives, and our world. We must put the Word of God in our heart with the Love of Jesus in our soul, let your soul shine, so we can become born again or saved Christians before the coming Rapture. Those Christians who have trusted Christ as their personal Lord and Savior will escape God's many horrible and terrible wraths during those three and half years of the Great Tribulation. This is the main reason for the church must reach out to the unsaved ones. Otherwise, the unsaved will miss the Rapture being left behind.

All the signs have been fulfilled for the Rapture. God's big heavenly time-clock is ticking away of the near coming Jesus for His Church. That time is much closer to high noon in America, or somewhere else in the world it's closer to the midnight hour. Let's be working for our Lord Jesus up to the time when our Lord will be taking away all Christians up in the big sky to be with Him in the Heaven of all heavens. Brothers and Sisters in Christ always be looking up, always be ready, and always be watching all the time. That time is so much nearer now than ever before when Christ will be coming for His Church. Jesus Christ will come like a thief in the night when everyone is not ready and watching. Our Lord Jesus Christ is the only Savior, the only Shepherd, and the only Son of God in the whole wide world. Only thru our Savior is the only way for our salvation. It's the only thing in this whole wide world, that is a free gift. The way to the cross leads to our Lord Jesus Christ for our salvation, then it leads us to heaven. Keep looking up all the time as our Lord Jesus be coming in the clouds to take all Christians to their heavenly home. Recalling a story in the Bible regarding who is ready by watching and who is not ready and watching for our Lord Jesus be coming for His church. It's the Parable of the Ten Virgins as told by Jesus.

> The kingdom of heaven will be like ten virgins who took their lamps and went out to meet the bridegroom. Five of them were foolish and five of them were wise. The foolish ones took their lamps but did not take any oil with them. The wise ones took oil in jars along with their lamps. The bridegroom was long time in coming and the ten virgins fell asleep. At midnight the cry rang out. Here is the bridegroom! Come out to meet him. Then the ten virgins woke up and trimmed their lamps. The foolish ones lamps were going out and was out of oil. While they on the way buy

oil, the bridegroom arrived. The virgins who was ready went in with him to the wedding banquet. And the door was shut. The foolish virgins came and could not enter for they knock on the door.

They cry out to open the door. His reply I tell you the truth I don't know you. Therefore, keep watch, because you do not know the day or the hour.

(Matthew 25:1-13)

That time is like the spring planting season for finding the unsaved people and then later it will be the harvest season time getting the unsaved people become Christians in the Lord Jesus. Those unsaved people, are now born again, will have the Holy Spirit in their heart and be ready for the Rapture. Everyone knows an unsaved person, it might be your loved one or a friend, such a person needs salvation. During these uncertain times, only a church revival will become that greater outreaching of saving the unsaved ones so they can be with the Lord Jesus there in heaven. Let's rekindle those old revival fires in the name of our Lord Jesus Christ. He is our Lord and the only Salvation Savior for the whole wide world. Our America must be more faithful than ever during these uncertain times. Let's always be looking up, always be ready, and always be watching for God's calling for His Church to come home.

❡

During these end-times or the last days of this church age, we need encourage each other. God's people should not fight with one other over church denomination and doctrine difference. There in our heavenly home, we all be together as children of God with Lord Jesus being the Church. We are bound together by the shed blood of the Lord Jesus Christ for we are blood Brothers and Sisters in Christ Jesus. By going to church each Sunday, we will become as one body in our Lord Jesus. As the power of God's word will spread throughout the whole wide world if we only believe. During our life journey, we have special gifts and special talents by using our hands and mind, let's make every day count as we all work together for our Christ Jesus and the church during this church age. Let's get in step as we march off to Victory in the army for our Lord. Finally, be strong in the Lord in his mighty power.

> As long as it is day, we must do the work of
> him who sent me.
> Night is coming, when no one can work.
> While I am in the world,
> I am the light of the world.
> (John 8:4-5) ¶

Satan the devil and his demons been in this world for many centuries even from the time of Adam and Eve as the evil serpent by causing the downfall of man and woman. Now in the end times or last days of the church age, we must be stronger in the Lord because Satan the devil and his demons are more active for their evil times in this twenty-first century. They know for sure that their evil times has become shorter and running out for them. This spiritual battle having the full armor of God, we can fight Satan the devil and his demons anytime and anywhere in this dark evil world. Always have more faith submit yourself to God by taken your stand against these evil ones. Be alert and keep on praying as your Heavenly Father will provide the proper full armor for your protection and safety.

> Submit yourselves to God. Resist the devil,
> and he will flee from you.
> (James 4:7)

We don't know when our Lord Jesus will return, but we do know that He will come again. The Bible says only the Heavenly Father knows the exact date of the Savior's return. The Scriptures indicates that Christ will come when we least expected, just like thief in the night. Until that time, we should be living godly lives by waiting, watching, and working until Jesus comes for His Church. Come soon, Lord Jesus.

> Now when these begin to happen, look up and
> lift up your head because your redemption
> draws near.
> (Luke 21:28)

It might be like playing that game hide-go-seek when we were children years ago. As we are counting 1 to 10, saying those words "ready or not here I come." That will be true when Christ comes in the sky of the Rapture for His Church with the same words "ready or not here I come."

> All authority in heaven and on earth been
> given to me.
> Therefore go and make disciples of all nations,
> baptizing them in the of name of the Father

and of Son and of the Holy Spirit, and teach
them to obey everything I have commanded
you. And surely I am with you always, to the
very end of this age. I am coming soon.
(Matthew 28: 18-20)

IT TAKES TWO, GOD and YOU by keeping the Church
doors open.

THIRTEEN

Need Salvation Go To Heaven

My dear Brothers and Sisters in Christ, I will be sharing with you, your family, and your friends the reasons for being born again in order everyone can go to heaven and be with our Lord Jesus forever.

Now is the time change your life for the good, don't wait too long for the Lord Jesus could come today or tomorrow for His Church of the coming Rapture. Being born again or saved, Jesus will give you that blessed hope with new joy in your heart and the peace of mind from the Prince of Peace. Because Christ lives in you, there will be "showers of blessing" from heaven for you each day. Since Jesus is the light of the world, we should carry that light into our hearts, lives, and soul. The Lord is your deliverer, your fortress, and your friend. We have a friend in Jesus and He is your forever solid rock. He is standing on the solid rock for you, come to Him for your salvation for his banner over you is love. God know you before you were born and He has a home in the third heaven, the Heaven of all heavens, just for you.

It's up to each person of how and want to live their life, that of a believer in Christ Jesus for your heavenly home or the sins of Satan for that burning hell. The only future hope for everyone is your faith thru grace and love of Jesus for our living salvation. We are living on this earth a short time, maybe seventy or eighty years that is more or less in years for this is only our temporary home.

You are precious, God will never leave you and will answer your prayers. Just have faith as a small mustard seed, Jesus will take away those fears and worries in your life. Just look back in Moses time, God told him I will rain down manna and quail from heaven for your people to eat. Next for their thirst, He brought them water from a rock. Because of His love for you, our Lord will do anything for you and keep you as His special friend. God has many blessings and outstanding promises for anyone, anytime, and anywhere. Let's be standing on the solid rock of many promises by singing that ole gospel song written by R. Kelso Carter:

"Sanding on the Promises"

> Standing on the promises of Christ my king.
> I'm Standing, standing on the promises of my
> Lord and Savior.

Lord Jesus been there for you from the very day you were first born, the very day being born again, the very day of your salvation, and the very day of the Rapture being heaven bound. When you were first born you cry and the world rejoice. Years later by having that born again Christian life when you die, you will rejoice and the world will cry. It is through the blood of Jesus Christ that we are saved from our sins, those old sinful ways are forgiven and forgotten. Yes, something wonderful going happen to you today for Jesus of Nazareth is coming your way. He will give you abundance life, everlasting life, and eternal life. Just remember one thing in your life journey, it's never too late make that change for a better life. When Jesus died on the cross for our sins, He told those faithful believers these kind words of love.

"You are with me in Paradise."

There's Bible story of two men one going heaven of paradise and the other one going to hell of burning fire.

> There was a rich man who was dressed in purple and fine linen and lived in luxury every day. At his gate was laid a beggar name Lazarus, covered with sores and longing to eat what fell from the rich man's table. Even the dogs came and licked his sores. The time came when the beggar died and the angles carried him to Abraham's side. The rich man also died and was buried. In hell, where he was in torment, he looked up and saw Abraham far away, with Lazarus by his side.
>
> So he called out to him, Father Abraham, have pity on me and sent Lazarus to dip his finger in water and cool my tongue, because I am in agony in this fire.
>
> But Abraham replied, Son, remember that in your lifetime you received your good things, but now he is in comforted and you are in agony. And besides all this, between us and

you a great chasm has been fixed, so that those want to go from here to you cannot, nor can anyone cross over from there to us.
(Luke 16:19-26)

This Bible story about the rich man became a beggar in hell while the beggar became rich man in heaven. Be sure you are on the right road that leads to eternal life into the Heaven of all heavens. Only few will walk the narrow road leading into heaven narrow gate as our Salvation Savior is waiting with welcome arms. Always make sure that your treasures are in heaven and not of this earth.

Enter through the narrow gate. For wide is the gate and broad is the road that leads to destruction, and many enter through it. But small is the gate and narrow the road that leads to life, and few find it.
(Matthew 7:13-14)

Those who know your name trust in you, for you, Lord, have never forsake those who seek you.
(Psalm 9:10)

The Lord is my light and my salvation.
(Psalm 27: 1)

My souls find rest in the Lord along; my salvation comes from him. He along is my rock and my salvation; he is my fortress, I will never be shaken.
(Psalm 62: 1-2)

Know that the Lord is God. It is he who made us, and we are his; we are his people, the sheep of his pasture.
(Psalm 100:3)

For those who seek are led by the Spirit of God are the children of God.
(Romans 8:14)

If God is for us, who can be against us?
He who did not spare his own Son, but gave him up for us all—how will he not also, along with him, graciously give us all things.
(Romans 8:31-32)

Seek ye first the kingdom of God, and his rightness.
(Matthew 6:33)

I tell you the truth, no one can see the kingdom of God unless he is born again."
(John 3: 3)

For God so loved the world that he gave his one and only son that whoever believes in him shall not perish but have eternal life."
(John 3:16)

Whoever believes in the Son has eternal life, but whoever rejects the Son will not see life, or God's wrath remains on him.
(John 3:36)

I am the way and the truth and the life.
No one comes to the Father except through me.
(John 14: 6)

Here I am! I stand at the door and knock.
If anyone hears my voice and opens the door,
I will come in and eat with that person and
they with me.
(Revelation 3:20)

Salvation is the greatest free gift for it give everyone that victory over their sins. To receive it, all you have to do is trust in Lord Jesus as your Savior. First, acknowledge and confess that you have sinned against God, that you are a sinner. Second, renounce your sins and do not go back your old ways of living. Third, by your faith you will receive Jesus Christ into your heart and life. It's always best to surrender completely to Him early in life, so you can have more wonderful joy and living peace. At the moment you receive the Lord as your Savior in your life, you will have all the hopes and joy in your heart, life, mind, and soul for rest of your life. Life journey will not be easy, but rewarding of having our Lord Jesus in your life.

Sin will keep you from your Bible, and your
Bible will keep you from sin.
old Quarter saying

It is true in this new twenty-first century as in the days and times of our Lord Jesus over two thousand years ago, you will seek Him and you will find Him. When you repent your life for your salvation, God will change your life by blessing you with much-joy in your body, heart, life, mind, and soul. With Him in our hearts we can live for Him by carrying His cross of reaching out with greater hope, more joy, and much love of Jesus onto the ones we love. Jesus lives in us so we can live in Him and live for Him.

> Seek me and you shall live.
> (Amos 5:4)

> From that time on Jesus began to preach. Repent, for the kingdom of heaven is near.
> (Matthew 4: 17)

> Repent, then, and turn to God, so that your sins maybe wiped out, and times of refreshing may come from God.
> (Acts 3:19)

> You must turn to God in repentance and have faith in our Lord Jesus.
> (Acts 20:21)

> That you confess with your mouth, "Jesus is Lord" and believe in your heart, that God raised him from the dead, you will be saved.
> (Romans 10:9)

> That Christ will dwell in your heart thru faith.
> (Ephesians 3:17)

Always remember God doesn't run away from sinners, He run toward them. Another way of saying this it's not running from sin, it's about running to God for your salvation. If we place our faith in Jesus Christ, we know absolute sure that we will have that heavenly eternal life. All you have to do is just get on your knees and pray in Jesus name with these words with your heart, mind, and soul.

> O God, I am a sinner and want to turn away from my sinful life. I believe that Jesus Christ is your Son for He died on the cross for my sins and you raised Him from the dead. I want Him as my Savior forever and forever more. Lord Jesus come into my life for my salvation and fill me with your Holy Spirit in Jesus name, amen.

> When they call on me, I will answer, I will be with them in trouble, I will rescue and honor them with a long life and give them my salvation.
> (Psalm 91:15-16)

Praise the Lord, I saw the light and let your light shine by sharing the good news of our Lord Jesus Christ.

> The Lord is my light, and my salvation—whom shall I fear.
> (Psalm 7:1)

It will be a new beginning with a new start for your life, for your own family, relatives, and friends. They will see a bigger change in your life with your new faith, hope, love, and peace. Your life with Lord Jesus will shine brighter than ever and even more in the years yet to come. Peace does not dwell in outward things but within the Soul. Let your soul shine. Being born again or saved, you will become one of God's children. Not the will of man but by the will of God and the willing of God by providing your salvation with your faith thru grace and love of Jesus. You will be joyful saying these words "The cross before me, the world behind me." Our goal and purpose in our life journey as our Father ordain and help us is to grow in Jesus Christ's love and become who He wants us to become by sharing the Gospel for Salvation to our love ones. Our Lord Jesus died over two thousand years ago as our Savior, we must Praised Him every day for He is the only Salvation Savior.

> This is how we know we are in him: who claims to live in him must walk as Jesus did. (1 John 2:5-6)

> Praise the Lord, praise the Lord, Let the earth hear His voice. Praise the Lord, praise the Lord, Let the people rejoice! O come to the Father thro' Jesus the Son, And give Him the glory; great things He has done.
> Fanny Crosby

Years ago in one of Rev. Moody's revival services reported stating these words "Two and one-half conversions." Someone asked him, "I suppose you mean two adults and one child." "No," Rev. Moody replied. "I mean two children and one adult. The children can give their whole lives to God, but an adult has only half a life to give."

Our salvation will be like the music and words of the song by Katherine Haney:

"I Love to Tell the Story."

> I love to tell the story, For some have never heard. The message of salvation from God's own holy Word.

> The Lord is my light and my salvation—whom shall I fear? The Lord is the stronghold of my life—of whom shall I be afraid?
> (Psalm 27: 1)

> One thing I ask of the Lord, this is what I seek: that I may dell in the house of the Lord all the days of my life.
> (Psalm 27:4)

> Enter the gates of thanksgiving and his courts with praise; give thanks to him and praise his name. For the Lord is good and his love endures forever, his faithfulness through all generations.
> (Psalm 100 4-5)

> You will keep in perfect peace him whose mind is steadfast, because he trusts in you. Trust in the Lord forever, for the Lord, the Lord, is the Rock eternal.
> (Isaiah 26: 3-4)

I gave them eternal life, and they shall never perish; no one can snatch them out of my hand.
(John 10: 28)

Salvation is found in no one, for there is no other name under heaven given to men my which we must be saved.
(Acts 4:12)

That you confess with your mouth, Jesus is Lord, and believe in your heart that God raise him from the dead, you will be saved. For it is your heart that you believe and are justified, and is from you're your mouth you confess and are saved.
(Romans 10:9-10)

Therefore, if anyone is in Christ, he is a new creation; the old has gone, the new has come.
(2 Corinthians 2:17)

Because of his great love for us, God, who is rich in mercy, made us alive with Christ even when we were dead in transgressions, it is by grace you have been saved. And God raised us up with Christ and seated us with him in heavenly realms in Christ Jesus, in order that in the coming ages he might show the incomparable riches of his grace, expressed in his kindness to us in Christ Jesus.
(Ephesians 2:4-7)

DON W. ROBERTSON

Behold I have open a door for you. I have set
open a door for you, and no man will be able
to close it.
(Revelation 3:8)

God will hear your prayer for your salvation, for the
Spirit of God will come into your heart, life, and soul with
greater love and greater peace of mind. The good news your
eternal life from your Heavenly Father begins right after your
salvation prayer. He will give you that newer heart and put
newer spirit in your life that will last forever. Even you are
lying on your deathbed or sickbed and you never made your
peace with God, it is still not too late. The dying thief on the
cross turned to Jesus Christ Jesus and said these words:

Lord, remember me. And Jesus replied,
Today you will be with me in Paradise.
(Luke 23: 42-43)

Just as soon you repent of your sins, you have received
Jesus Christ as your Savior, then your name will be written
in the Lamb's Book of Life. There is a strong relationship
having Your faith for your salvation and later being baptized.
Being baptized with the Holy Spirit is a blessing for you
as you come out of that living water as a new person, that
was true with my living water baptism. Having both your
salvation and being baptized will become a double blessing.
Being baptized is not required of going to heaven. My three
children were baptized during their mother, my first wife,
memorable services at our First Christian Church, it was a
nice wonderful blessing. As their mother looking down from
heaven that day of her special services being pleased and

proud seeing her children being baptized. Our family are proud for each other as we stay together with love for those plans and purpose what our Heavenly Father has for us to do all in His Glory. What this day holds for us and how long this life's journey will last for we don't know for sure? Because He lives, we can face tomorrow. Just live one day at a time as we talk and walk each day with our Lord Jesus.

> I baptize you with water for repentance.
> But after me will come one who is more powerful than I, He will baptize you with the Holly Spirit and fire. Then Jesus came from Galilee to the Jordan to be baptize by John.
> As soon Jesus was baptized, he went up out of the water, at that moment heaven was opened, and he saw the Spirit of God.
> And a voice from heaven said, "This is my Son, whom I love; with Him I am well please."
> (Matthew 3:11,13, 16-17)

> Therefore go and make disciples of all nations, baptizing them in the name of the Father and of the Son and of the Holy Spirit, and teaching them to obey everything I have commanded you. And surely I am with you always, to the very end of the age.
> (Matthew 28:19-20)

> Whoever believes and is baptized will be saved, but whoever does not believe will be condemned.
> (Mark 16:16)

John, the Baptist, went into all he country around the Jordan, preaching a baptism of repentance for the forgiveness of sins.
(Luke 3:3)

Jesus was gaining and baptizing more disciples than John, although in fact it was not Jesus who baptized, but his disciples.
(John 4:1-2)

I am the gate; whoever enters through will be saved.
He will come in and go out, and find pastures.
(John 10:9)

For God says, "In the time of my favor I heard you, and in the day of salvation I help you."
I tell you, now is the time of God's favor, now is the time for salvation.
(2 Corinthians 6:1)

You are all sons of God through faith in Christ Jesus, for all of you who baptized into Christ have clothed yourself in Christ.
(Galatians 3:26-27)

For it is by grace you have been saved, through faith and this is not from yourselves, it is a gift from God—not by works, so that no one can boast.
(Ephesians 2: 8-9)

Because of the death and resurrection of Jesus Christ, with our faith and by His grace and love we can be born again or saved for our salvation. Your sins will be forgiven and forgotten as we become one of God's children. Our Lord Jesus Christ as our Savior will reach out to us in love so we can reach out to Him with love. Every Christian is born twice: first physically born into our earthly family and then spiritually born into a family of God.

> May the God of hope fill you with all joy and peace as you trust in him, so that you may overflow with hope by the power of the Holy Spirit.
> (Romans 15:13)

> May our Lord Jesus Christ himself and God our Father, who love us and by his grace gave us eternal encouragement agreement and good hope, encourage your hearts and strengthen you in every good deed and word.
> (2 Thessalonians 2:16-17)

> Here I am! I stand at the door and knock, if any man hears my voice, and open the door, I will come in.
> (Revelation 3:20)

Thank you Lord Jesus for our Salvation, later being together in Your Paradise. What a Blessing of all blessings, what a Promise off all promises for this blessing free gift from our dear Lord Jesus Christ. Being born again or being saved is by our faith thru the grace and love of Jesus is the only way for a person going to heaven. It's an awesome power by praising our Lord for our salvation. Praise the Lord and rejoice always for it brings much joy and greater peace into our life, our mind, and our soul. We don't earn or work our way into heaven for it's a free gift from God thru His Son, our Lord Jesus Christ. We must believe with our faith every day by reaching out to others with the love of Jesus. Some glad morning when our life's journey is over, we will fly away in glory as our Heavenly Father and our Lord Jesus will welcome us with open arms to our heavenly home.

> In his great mercy he has given us a new birth into a living hope through the resurrection of Jesus Christ from the dead, and into an inheritance that can never perish, spoil, or fade-kept in heaven for you, who through faith is shielded by God's power until the coming of the salvation that is ready be revealed. You were redeemed with the precious blood of Jesus. Through him you believed in God, who raised him from the dead and glorified him, and so your faith and hope are in God. Now that you have purified your-selves by obeying the truth so that you have sincere love for your bothers, love one another deeply from the heart. For you have been born again, not of perishable seed, but of imperishable, through the living and enduring word of God. "All men are like grass, and all their glory is like the flowers in the field; the grass withers and the flowers fall, but the word of the Lord stands forever."
> (1Peter 1: 3-5, 18-19, 21-25)

During our life journey without challenges, we never learn new skills or gain spiritual strength in order to endure. As faithful God's children, we can be His Lighthouse with our helping hands to carry His cross by being a faithful good neighbor in need. Always rejoice and be glad in it for our brighter hopes, greater joy, much love, for being His lighthouse. During this wonderful life's journey of eighty-nine, now the "golden years," my calling from God is doing the following five L's:

laboring, learning, listing, living, and loving for my Lord Jesus.

> Love you, O Lord, my strength. The Lord is my rock, my fortress and my deliverer, my God is my rock, in whom I take refuge. He is my shield and the horn of my salvation, my stronghold. I call to the Lord, who is worthy of my praise and I am save.
> (Psalm 18: 1-2)

> Even to your old age and gray hairs I am he, I am he who will sustain you. I have made you and I will carry you; and I will rescue you.
> (Isaiah 46: 4)

> May the God of hope fill you with all joy and peace as you trust him, so that may overflow with hope by the power of the Holy Spirit.
> (Romans 15:13)

> Now faith is being sure of what we hope for and certain of what we do not see.
> (Hebrews 11:1)

Because of our salvation, which only takes place once in our life time thru the grace and love by our Lord Jesus. Everyone was first born as a baby in our mother's womb and born again the second time has God's children. Our Lord Jesus wrote our name in the Lamb Book of Life being heaven bound. Because He lives, we can live for our Lord Jesus by counting our blessings knowing for sure as we face tomorrow many unknowns. Let's sing these two songs all together: parts of "Because He Lives," and "Count Your Blessings."

> Because He lives I can face tomorrow,
> Because He lives all fear is gone:
> Because I know He holds the future,
> And life is worth the living just because He lives.
>
> Count your blessings; name them one by one. Count your many blessings; see what God has done.
>
> Everyone whose name is found written in the Book of Life—will be delivered. Multitudes who sleep in the dust of the earth will awake: some to everlasting life, others to shame and everlasting contempt. Those who are wise will shine like the brightness of the heavens, and those who lead many to righteousness, like the stars for ever and ever.
> (Daniel 12:1-3)
>
> In my Father's house are many rooms, if it was not so, I would tell you so. I am going there

to prepare a place for you. And if I go and prepare a place for you, I will come back, and take you with me that will you always may be where I am.
(John 14:2-3)

Our citizenship is in heaven. And we eagerly await a Savor from there, the Lord Jesus Christ, who, by the power that enables him to bring everything under his control, will transform our lowly bodies so that they will be like his glorious body.
(Philippians 3:20-21)

IT TAKES TWO, GOD and YOU for our Salvation and sharing the Gospel.

FOURTEEN

The Blessed Hope

In our own America there are few churches that's preaching and teaching about the end times or the last days and the Rapture of His church. This must change or it might be too late as many unsaved people being left behind of not going to heaven. The coming of the Lord Jesus for His Church of the Rapture is not myth for itis the real fact. As we approach the final ending of this church age, there are many questions being asked "Will the born again or those saved Christians be going thru the Tribulation?" There are three major views among Bible Pastors and the church:

- The post-tribulation position states that the church is going thru all the Tribulation.
- The mid-tribulation position states that the church is going thru the first half of the Tribulation.
- The pre-tribulation position states that the church will not go thru any of the Tribulation.

According to the Bible only the pre-tribulation is true as stated the book 1stThessalionians and other related Bible verses.

> Brothers, we do not want be ignorant about those who fall asleep or to grieve like rest of men, who have no hope.
> We believe that Jesus died and rose again and so we believe that God will bring with Jesus those who have fallen asleep in him.
> According to the Lord's own word, we tell you that we are who are still alive, and who are left till the coming of the Lord, will certainly not precede those who have fallen asleep.
> For the Lord himself will come down from heaven, with a loud command, with the voice of the archangel and with the trumpet call of God, and the dead in Christ will rise first. After that, we who are still alive and are left will be caught up together with them in the clouds to meet the Lord in the air. And so we will be with the Lord forever. Therefore encourage each other with these words. (1Thessalonians 4: 13-18)

His calling of the Rapture will be like "twinkling of an eye" which is less than a faction of one second. As God lay us down to sleep, real soon the Lord will awake us with His command. With that loud command from the Lord, I can just hear Him saying "Come up here My Brothers and Sisters for I' am taken you to your heavenly home." The loud command is a word used by the military as a direct order. The voice of the archangel which is Michael because angels are God's messengers. The trumpet calling of God to announce the appearance of royalty which is our Lord Jesus Christ being the King of kings and the Lord of lords. This will be the last trumpet blast for all those born again Brothers and Sisters of Christs. Always keep looking up, always be ready, and always be watching for His coming which is very soon.

¶

Men of Galilee, "why do you stand here looking into the sky"
This same Jesus, who has been taken from you into heaven, will come back in the same way you have seen him go into heaven."
(Acts 1:11)

By his power God raised the Lord from the dead, and he will raise us also.
(1Corinthians 6:14)

Listen, I will tell you a mystery: We all will not sleep, but we all be changed—in a flash, in the twinkling of an eye,
¶For the trumpet will sound, the dead will be raised imperishable, and we will be changed.
Death have been swallow up in victory.
(1Corinthians 15: 51-52, 54)

At this time I will share with you a touching poem written by Robert Frost.

"Stopping by the Woods on a Snowy Evening"

Whose woods these I think I know.
His house is in the village though;
my little must think it queer he will not see
me stopping here to watch his woods fill up
with snow to stop without a farmhouse near
between the woods and frozen lake the darkest
evening of the year.
He gives his harness bells a shake to ask if
there is some mistake.
The only other sound's the sweep of easy wind
and downy flake.
The woods are lovely, dark and deep, but I
have promise to keep, and miles to go before
I sleep,
And miles to go before I sleep.

No one known about that day or hour, not
even the angels in heaven, nor the Son, but
only the Father. As it was in the days of Noah,
so it will be the coming of the Son of Man.
Two men will be in the field; one will be taken
and the other one left. Two women will be
grinding with a hand mill: one will be taken
and the other one will be left.
(Matthew 24: 36-37, 40-41)

So you also must be ready, because the Son of
Man will come at an hour you do not expect him.
(Matthew 24:44)

For a time is coming when all who are in their graves will hear his voice and will come out—those who have done good will rise to live, and those who done evil will be condemned.
(John 5:28-29)

For my Father's will that everyone who looks to the Son and believes in him shall have eternal life, and I will raise him up at the last day.
(John 6:40)

I am the resurrection and the life. He who believes in me will live, even though he dies; and whoever lives and believes in me will never die.
(John 11:25-26)

The trumpet will sound, and the dead will be raised imperishable, and we will be change.
(1 Corinthians 15:52)

We know that the one raised the Lord Jesus from the dead will raise us with Jesus and present us with you in his present.
(2 Corinthians 4:14)

The blessed hope during this blessed church age will be the near coming of the Rapture for all God's Children. The blessed hope for Israel is the second coming of her Messiah, their Lord Jesus Christ. The blessed hope for the world is the near coming of our Lord Jesus for He will do this in the Glory of His Heavenly Father. That time is more apparent now than any time in our lives for His near coming of the Rapture. Be patient and stand firm for the Lord Jesus Christ will come in all His glorious appearing. Hallelujah, we are not along for He is our Christ, champion, comforter, companion, and counselor.

While we wait for the "blessed hope" the glorious appearing of our great God and Savior, Jesus Christ.
Titus 2:13)

Be patient, then brothers and sisters until the Lord's coming. You too, be patient stand firm, because the Lord is coming near.
(James 5: 7-8)

Grace and peace be yours in abundance.
Praise be to the God and Father of our Lord Jesus Christ! In his great mercy he has given us a new birth into a living hope through the resurrection of Jesus Christ from the dead, and into an inheritance that can never perish, spoil or fade—keep in heaven for you.
(1 Peter 1: 2-4)

All men are like grass, and all their glory is like the flowers in the field; the grass withers and the flowers fall, but the word of God stands forever.
(1 Peter 1:24)

But the day of the Lord will come like a thief.

What kind of people you ought to be? You ought to live holy and godly lives as you look forward to the day of God and speed of his coming.
(2 Peter 3:10-11)

Dear children, continue in him, so when he appears we may be confident and unashamed before of his coming.
If you know that he is righteous, you know that everyone who does right has been born of him.
(1 John 2:28-29)

Dear friends, now we are children of God, and what we will be has not yet been made known. But we know that when he appears, we shall be like him, for we shall see him as he is.
(1 John 3:2)

When the Lord return for the Rapture, those dead in Christ will be caught up first. After that, those born again people who are still alive will be caught up and be with them in the sky. Heir of our Salvation will become blessed assurance, Jesus is mine, blessed assurance for Jesus is my Savior. In the resurrection morning we will shall meet Him in the big sky with our new glorified bodies. All faithful Christians, those born again, will be living together with the Lord Jesus in the third-heaven which is the Heaven of all heavens. Our Lord Jesus gives us comforting blessed assurance that all God's people will be together in the Heaven of all heavens be

Praising Him all day long. Our Lord Jesus has won the battle over death with a Hallelujah Victory as all faithful believers shall rise in victory all because of the risen Christ. It will be like that old joyful gospel song written many years ago by Fanny Crosby:

"Blessed Assurance, Jesus is Mine"

> Blessed assurance, Jesus is mine! Oh, what a foretaste of glory divined! Heir of salvation, purchase of God, Born of His spirit, wash in His blood. This is my story, this is my song Praising my Savior all the day long; This is my story, this is my song, Praising my Savior all the day long.

ʃ

When we die our body's spirit and soul will go to the third heaven. After the Rapture of the Church, we will have glorified new body just like our Lord Jesus when he went back to heaven at the age of thirty-three. Our new bodies will be health free with a sound mind and being young again at the same age of thirty-three as our Lord Jesus Christ.

It will be alike the stages of a new butterfly. The butterfly life cycle begins when a caterpillar spins cocoon around itself, later become a new glorified new butterfly. Just as a butterfly, it will be like that Gospel song "I will fly away"

What a day that will be during the Rapture with God's calling by saying "My children come home for it 's supper time." The third Heaven is a real place and our citizenship will be in this Heaven of all heavens. Jesus is a great authority of heaven, He came from heaven to earth as the Savior for our salvation and then return back to heaven as King of kings. During these last 2,000 years, He is preparing our eternity heavenly home that of the New Jerusalem of many mansions.

> The day of death better than the day of birth.
> (Ecclesiastes 7:1)

> In my Father's house are many rooms; if it was not so, I would have told you.
> I am going there to prepare a place for you.
> And if I go and prepare a place for you, I will come back and take you to be with me that you also may be where I am.
> (John 14: 2-3)

> But our citizenship is in heaven. And we eagerly await a Savor from there, the Lord Jesus, who, by the power that enables him to bring everything under his control, will transform us our lowly bodies so that they will be like his glorious body.
> (Philippians 3:20-21)

There is a true story how God change the life of this man, let's take a look together of what happen:

A Union general in the Civil War, Lew Wallace from Indiana, also set out to write a book disapproving the deity of Jesus Christ and His resurrection. He ended up defending it in his famous book "Ben-Hur," the most influential book of the nineteen century. Several years later Hollywood made a great movie regarding this book.

Your redeemer loves you always and you can spend eternity with your love-ones in heaven.

> The Lord is my shepherd, I shall not want.
> (Psalm 23:1)

> The most thrilling thing about heaven is that Jesus Christ will be there. I will see Him face to face.
> Billy Graham

The people of this old world need our Lord Jesus for He will give us a new song in our heart. Let's rejoice together that ole favorite gospel song written by E. E Hewitt:

"When We All Get to Heaven."

> When we all get to heaven.
> What a day of rejoicing that will be!
> When we all see Jesus, We'll sing and shout the victory!

> He who testifies to these things says, "Yes, I am coming soon."
> Amen, Come, Lord Jesus.
> The grace of the Lord Jesus be with God's people. Amen.
> (Revelation 22: 20-21)

IT TAKES TWO, GOD and YOU, keep looking up, be ready, and be watching for the coming Rapture.

FIFTEEN

Last Days Signs

God has a plan and a purpose for our life, even while we are still in our mother's womb. It is up everyone how to lived up to those plans and purpose. The next few chapters informed those unsaved people regarding the signs of the end times or the last days what will happen after the Rapture of the Church and the coming wraths of God. After all the Christians have died, our bodies will rest in the ground or at sea and by means of cremation those ashes will be saved and be united. Then our souls and spirits will go into the presence of our Lord Jesus in His Paradise which is the third heaven. After the Rapture all Christians will be caught up in the air with Lord Jesus and being escorted by our Lord Jesus and His Angels. This will become a life time one-way journey, the only one like it. We will be living forever with our Lord Jesus Christ in our heavenly home with glorified new bodies just like the glorified body of our Lord Jesus. You are in heaven because you are born again by your faith with the blessing promise by our Lord Jesus. While all Christians are living the good life in the Heaven of heavens. What will happen to all the unsaved people left behind that miss the Rapture?

Because the Bible is 25 percent prophetic and being absolutely accurate, we should study the Bible for the sure Word. It gives all faithful Christians that living peace in their heart and peaceful mind that they going to heaven after the Rapture of His church. God's Blessings for anyone that reads and those hear the words of this prophecy.

One way of looking at the book of Revelation it is a roadway map of the future. God has given the people of the world many warnings thru out the Bible regarding the future events. Any unsaved person should be aware and take notice about the three evil ones that be coming into this dark evil old world. These are Satan the devil, the Antichrist known as the beast, and the False Prophet. Next will be the seven years known as the Tribulation with the last half of those seven years will be the terrible Great Tribulation. Jesus said "all things are the beginning of birth pains," that is how the Great Tribulation will become. The upcoming events in the Bible is not a fairy tale, nor a myth for it's the real true coming event.

The only way for anyone's salvation is thru our faith with the grace and love of our Lord Jesus Christ, then we will become God's children. It's most important that everyone be ready and watch for His coming for it could happen soon and it will be soon.

Pastors must preached their sermons and teach in the Sunday school classes what God wants your church need to hear and learn, that is the sure Word of God. Preachers give us that "Ole Time Religion for it's good enough for me and for my Brothers and Sisters in Christ." The mission of the church is to be the lighthouse by taken the Gospel of salvation to all the world where there is no hope. More than ever in this twenty-first century the people in America and those living in other parts the world need the blessed hope of salvation in their lives. The Church and all Christians are being attacked every day of each year by Satan the devil and his demons with no end in sight. This is only one of many reasons to spread the gospel where it is most needed.

> Preach the Word. For the time will come when
> my will not put up with sound doctrine.
> Instead suit their own desires, they will gather
> around them in great number teachers to say
> what their itching ears want to hear. They will
> turn away the truth and turn aside to myths.
> (2 Timothy 4: 2-4)

Look what Christ said to John the Apostle about the seven churches of Asia Manor found in the book of Revelation. Because of that John wrote letters to those seven churches for them to stand firm in their faith. John was mostly concern with the lukewarm church of Laodicea. Some TV prophecy preachers today are saying many churches in America have become lukewarm. Do you believe that some or most churches have become lukewarm, how about your church? The Bible states there will be a great "falling away" from the faith and truth. Wake up church this falling away is now more than ever.

> So because you are lukewarm—neither hot nor
> cold—I am about to spit you out of my mouth.
> (Revelation 1:16)

You say that you are rich and have acquired
wealth and do not need a thing.
But you do not realized that you are wretched,
pitiful, poor, blind, and naked.
(Revelation 3:17)

Whoever has ears, let them hear what the
Spirit says to the churches.
(Revelation 3:22)

Those seven churches many hundred years ago or even
some people in church today of this twenty-first century
don't believe there is a falling away of the church or their
church is lukewarm. There are many people not accepting
Jesus as their Lord and Savior. We are seeing all the signs of
end times or the last day today in this twenty-first century.
Some people today are failing to see those end time signs or
don't believed it going to happen. What are the signs of the
end of age?

We have heard or seen predictions of the so-called
dooms days in the past years. It was the Y2K panic of
the year 1999 when people of the world had fears as the
calendar was shifting into the new century of the year 2000.
Experts predicted that all computers would quite working at
midnight of the old year 1999. Many people were stocking
up on food, medical supplies, and water for the preparing
of the worldwide collapse. Take a wild guest what really
did happen, yes, you are right, this old world still the same.
What doom-times are next to happen to our world, maybe
like that of December 21, 2012. It was mostly based upon
the Maya people calendar over 5,125 years ago by using

astrology rather than faith regarding the last days on earth. It was the same date that the Hopi Indians of the Southwest United States. Likewise, it was the same predictions and visions from Nostradamus over 500 years ago. It seems strange, that we were getting those same three predications of the future dreadful coming events regarding the same date of December 21, 2012. That date has come and gone, the world of sins is still the same, maybe gotten worst. Than on August 2018, the History TV channel had a program regarding the present 112th Pope Francis would be the last Pope before the end of this Church age. The Bible states be aware these kind of predictions, many have come and gone without any truth in them.

We have heard or seen other dates and predictions of the so-called doomsday. We will see more of these same kind doomsday predictions in the future. Not the angels or the Son of God, don't know the final end date of this church age. Only our Heavenly Father has the real and true answers regarding the dates and times for the end-times of His Church. Just keep on believing the words of God for He holds the whole world in His hands. What does the word of God in the Bible tells us about the end-times or the last days? Let's take a look together at His words.

> Therefore keep watch, because you don't know
> the day or the hour.
> (Matthew 25:13)

These are the words by Jesus as He was talking to His disciples on the Mount of Olives.

Watch out that no one deceives you.

For many will come in my name, claiming I am the Christ. You will hear of war and rumors of wars. Nation will rise against nations, and kingdom against kingdoms. There will be famines and earthquakes in various places.

Many will turn away from the faith and will betray and hate each other. Because of the increase of wickedness, the love of most will turn cold, but he who stands firm to the end will be saved. And the Gospel of the kingdom will be preached in the whole world as a testimony to all nations and then the end will come.
(Matthew 24: 4-14)

These are the beginning of birth pains.
(Mark 13;8)

Look at the fig tree and all the trees. When they sprout leaves, you can see for yourselves and know that summer is near.

Even so, when you see these things happening, you know that the kingdom of God is near. Be always on the watch, and pray that you may be able to escape all that is about to happen, and that you may be able to stand before the Son of Man.
(Luke 21:29-31, 36)

In the end times or the last days of this church age, we will see knowledge being increased. It's happening more than ever, technology is moving fast and faster. Greater

DON W. ROBERTSON

information, knowledge, and technology are more available today than ever before. We are more advance and educated in advanced communication, international finance, better medical care, stronger military power, the space program, faster transportation, and the list goes on and on. The final end will not come before everyone in the world, every man, woman, and child has the opportunity to hear the Gospel. All the signs of the last days or the end times are happening Now.

> The Lord gives wisdom, and from his mouth comes knowledge and understanding.
> (Proverbs 2:6)

> But the word of God continued to increase and spread.
> (Acts 12:24)

> The first time in history, we have the technology to preach the Gospel to every tribe, every tongue, and every nation.
> Billy Graham

In this new twenty-first century as I am writing this book of the year 2023-2024, we are seeing all the signs have taken placed. We are witnessing exactly what our God said in the Bible would take place in this church age. The following are some facts our nation and the world will be seeing: being deceived by people, surge of deadly disaster, many earthquakes thru out the world, massive hurricanes, and rumors of wars.

We are living in the last of the last days.

The reporting by Fox News, the cover-ups of Secretary of State Hillary Clinton when she erase all those so-call classified e-mails. How the dishonest D Party of the 2020 Presidential National Election stealing votes by means of fraud from President Trump and those same votes from the America's GOP voters. Why did both Forty-fourth and the Forty-sixth Presidents transforming America's economy and our ways of life with socialism? How dishonest was the Biden family's several millions dollars involvement with China/Ukraine? It's hard believe that some leaders in Washington D.C. will deceived the people of our country just for money and wanting more power. We elected people for our country on Capitol Hill with their big promises which later become broken promises. Those political people spent most of their time arguing and fighting between themselves and wanting be re-elected. We are hearing those big lies for America and seeing the people being deceived again and more again. Prayer is the only answer so that our Heavenly Father will give those political people knowledge, understanding, wisdom, and a greater love for our America.

Over 150 years ago the American Indians had a good saying to America: "The great white father in Washington speaks with forked tongue." Those politicians in Washington D. C. still today "speak with forked tongues" with the people's viewpoint with words like "We don't trust you anymore." Sound like lots of double talk.

Don't think you are immune to money investment schemes with your business and education background. Everyone can easy fall into a financial trap by clever con peoples. People like Bernie Madoff with his Ponzi scheme by taken advantage and deceived many thousands of peoples. He was using their life-time savings with promises for bigger return on their investments which never happen. While

Bernie Madoff was living the rich and famous life-style. Because of those broken big return investment promises, those hurting people were saying "What are we going to do now for we are too old start over again." When it sounds too good that is the reason to back off and run away fast. Those dreams and hopes for your "golden years" retirement money can turn into big nightmare. Always check with the Better Business Bureau (BBB) for their honest advice. There are many faithful honest money managers, investments thru banks or insurance companies, and mutual funds like Vanguard or investments firms like Raymond James will take care your retirement golden years.

> There will be terrible times in the last days.
> People will be lovers of themselves, lovers of
> money, boastful proud, abusive, disobedient to
> their parents, ungrateful, unholy, without love,
> unforgiving, slanderous, without self-control,
> brutal, not lovers of the good, treacherous,
> rash, conceited, lovers of pleasure, rather
> lovers of God.
> (2 Timothy 2:1-4)

We are seeing earthquakes where they never happened before and they are becoming stronger. Like the one in Mexico 2017, the worst one in the last one hundred years for that country. August 2021 Haiti earthquake killing over 2,000 as many 9,900 people injured with thousands homeless. The last few years there were several underwater earthquakes with powerful tsunami or major earthquakes around the world claiming several thousand people lives. Sometime in the future the real big earthquakes will take place along the Mississippi River and the California Coast with major property damage and people being killed by the thousands.

Within six weeks of each other in September 2017, there was three major hurricanes: Hurricane Harvey hitting Texas, Hurricane Irma hitting Florida, and it was Hurricane Marie hitting Puerto Rico. This was the deadly hurricane hitting Puerto Rico since 1900, with 2,975 people killed and many months later still in major ruined. August 2018 major Hurricane Lane hit the big Island plus the smaller ones of Hawaii. In some areas of the big island with rain over 3 feet causing major flooding and mudslides. September 2019 it was the very disastrous category 5 Hurricane Dorian hitting the Bahamas with almost 200 mph wind, major flooding resulting from heavy rain, and many hundreds people killed and missing. August, September, and October year 2020 with major Hurricanes Laura, Sally, and Delta causing major damage with heavy rain, major flooding, and tornadoes hitting the Gulf states with many people killed. It was very bad year of over seventy Atlantic storms, REMA stated "never faced a year like 2020."

August 2021 Category 5 Hurricane Ida hit New Orleans very hard leaving trail of destruction. Spring Year 2022 Hurricane Ian done major damage to Florida

March 2020 here in Putnam County, Tennessee, we had the worst EF4-tornado year in history causing major damage and destroyed 500 homes and killing 19 people. President Trump, Governor Lee, and local Mayors came with their blessing, concerns, and financial support. We are thankful for all the many helping hands that came out for the clean-ups. December 2021 with 44 terrible tornadoes hit 9 mid-west states, there in Kentucky the worst tornadoes in state history as some 76 people were killed mostly in the small town of Mayfield was complete leveled. March 2022 was the worst month on record of the number of tornados for our country, this is only the start of the tornado season.

August 2021 the nightmare major flood wiped-out the town of Waverly, Tennessee up 17 inches of rain fell in less twenty-four hours. Five hundred homes and business places damage or destroyed with 22 people were killed including baby twins.

The year 1980 the big volcano eruption of flowing ash maybe worst in America's history was Mount Saint Helens in Washington State which was unreal of major damage with many people killed. On average, natural disasters kill 60,000 people globally each year. December 2022 Hawaii volcano eruption with major lava flow.

Our America is seeing brutal wicked violence of many mass shootings and killings in churches, colleges, schools, various public and work places. There seems to be no end of these mass shootings and killings, each year they are getting more terrible. All mayors, governors, any president should be more concern for the protection and safety of our country by taken necessary action of solving these mass shootings and killings by having more trained police force, never defunding.

Over the years we have seen many wars and rumors of wars like the two horrible two world wars with the reign of murderous dictators. Our country was facing the war against North Korea and few years later, it was the Vietnam War. That sad day of 9/11 in NYC when two hijack planes crash into the NYC Twin Towers and a hijack plane crashed into the Pentagon, all these evil attacks were done on purpose.

The final war will become the battle of Armageddon which will be the War of all wars. Our Lord Jesus with His Saints will be riding on big white horses in glory for the final war of all times being won with the Word of God by the King of kings.

Trust in God which is the only real answer for He is in total control as our America facing many unknown conditions. For sure it takes More Faith by being less fearful.

> When I am afraid, I will trust in you. In God,
> whose word I praise, in God I trust; I will not
> be afraid. What can mortal man do to me.
> (Psalm 56: 3-4)

The Bible has given us many signs that we are living in the last days of His Church. We are thankful for both Christian radio and Christian TV stations with their faithful leaders and the preachers taken the Good News of the Gospel around the world for this will be the last sign of the end times or the last days of this Church age. This last sign is happening now in this twenty-first century, we should be more alert, keep looking up, be more ready, and be watching more than ever. All Christians will be full of joy and be rejoicing the day when our Lord Jesus be coming in the clouds for His Church.

> This gospel of the kingdom will be preached in
> the whole world as a testimony to all nations,
> and then the end will come.
> (Matthew 24:14)

Our Lord Jesus said, "When you see these things look up for your redemption drawing near."
(Luke 21:28)

The coming of the Lord Jesus Christ is the backbone and the heartbeat of Bible prophecy that is written in the books of Daniel and Revelation. My dear faithful Christian Brothers and Sisters, the Lord Jesus Christ will always be our King of kings and Lord of lords.

IT TAKES TWO, GOD and YOU, keep Looking up Jesus Christ is Coming soon.

SIXTEEN

The 3 Evil Ones

After the Rapture of the Church, those people left behind will be going through period of confusion what happened with great deal of fear. There will be breaking news day and night on all radio stations and TV stations. What happened and where are the missing people? Lots of what's, when's, where's, and why's questions, without answers. Chaotic madness times of looting, protesting, riots, shooting and killings. Under Socialism Government leadership, our America will never be the same again, the beginning of the end for America.

Those unsaved people will see seven hard and long years ahead of them known as the Tribulation. The last three and half years is known as the Great Tribulation will become the hardest and worst of all times without escape and relief. According to the Bible, this time period will be time and times and a half, same as 42 months or three and a half years. This seven-year period is also known as Daniel's 70 Weeks, the last seven weeks will become the Tribulation period. It will begin when the church age ends and the Rapture have already taken place. Please, take some time to read the books of Daniel and Ezekiel in the Bible. Most of this information of what will happened after the Rapture of His Church is taken from the book of Revelation.

> Blessed is the one who reads the words of this prophecy, and blessed are those who hear it and take it to heart what is written in it, because the time is near.
> (Revelation 1:3)

After the falling away of the church and the Rapture of His Church, it will be the beginning of the seven year Tribulation period. There will be the coming of the three evil ones known as Satan the devil, the Antichrist the beast, and the False Prophet spreading fear with many evil unknowns. Next will be the seven-year rule and the reign of this unholy trinity. During the Great Tribulation period of three and half years will be an outbreak of God's wrath consisting of darkness, death, destruction, judgment, lawlessness, and so many unknowns. The evil man of sin will appear which is the Antichrist, the general of Satan the devil. He is better known as the Beast or the Little Horn.

Like the days of Moses in Egypt of "Let my people go," many evil unsaved people of the Great Tribulation kept on blasphemed God in heaven. Those evil unsaved people with those harden hearts will not change from their sinful ways. It seems over those past many thousands of years, that man has not learned God's ways or the words of the Ten Commandments. Sound like that old sayings "What goes around comes around."

In the Revelation of Jesus, which God gave Him to show his servants what must take place. He made it known by sending his angel to his servant John the Apostle there on the Island of Patmos the year AD 96. God told John what you have seen, what is now, and what will take place later. These will be the Word of God and the testimony of our Lord Jesus Christ. The many wrath of God will be hard and tough against those evil unsaved people never be anything like it again. There are three main God's wrath for His judgments they are the following:

the Seal Judgments, the Trumpet Judgments, and the Bowl Judgments.

Only the Lamb, our Lord Jesus Christ, can open the seven Seals Judgment reveal the beginning many wrath of God. Consisting the Four Horsemen of the Apocalypse who will be galloping everywhere of bring world devastation. The first horseman is the Antichrist, who will be riding his white horse as a conqueror on conquest. The next horsemen be riding his fiery red horse, he was given power with a large sword to take peace away from the earth with war. The next horseman be riding his black horse, he is holding a pair of scales in his hand bring famine. The last horseman be riding his pale horse, he bring death from plague. Next, that of cosmic disorder of earthquakes, the sun will turn black, the moon will turn blood-red, and stars fall from the sky. The seven angels sounded the seven Trumpets Judgment for God's wrath consisting the following: hail and fire, third of earth be burn up, sea turned into blood, water turn bitter, and darkness of the moon, the stars, and the sun. The seven angels pour out their seven Bowls Judgement consisting: ugly and painful sores on people, the sea and drinking water turn into blood, the sun scotch people with fire, severe earthquakes, and a voice from heaven saying "it is done." Because of these three judgments, there will be nothing like this and never again.

> The Lord is a jealous and avenging God; the Lord takes vengeance and is fill with wrath. The Lord takes vengeance on his foes and maintains is wrath against his enemies. (Nahum 1:1-2)

> For then there will be great distress, unequaled from the beginning of the world until now and never again. (Matthew24:21)

> ¶ Men will faint from terror, apprehensive what is going on the world, for the heavenly bodies will be shaken. (Luke 21:26)

> I will pour out my Spirit in those days, and I will show wonders in heaven above and signs on earth below, blood and fire and billows of smoke. The sun will be turned to darkness and the moon to blood. (Acts 2:18-20)

The hardest and worst part of Daniels's 70 Weeks will the last three and half years known as the Great Tribulation. This will be the worst of times for those evil unsaved people ever have to face, those taken the mark 666 of the beast. There will be three evil ones that will be coming in the end times or the last days and they be running here and there by misleading the unsaved people. These three evil ones are Satan the devil, the Antichrist the beast, and the False Prophet. Satan is a fallen angel who wasn't satisfied worship God for he wanted to occupy his throne in heaven. This evil one has not changed and still is self- centered. The Antichrist will be the political leader of one world government and the False Prophet will be the spiritual leader of the world.

Just as there is a Holy Trinity, God the Father, Jesus Christ the Son, and the Holy Spirit. Also, we will find that Satan the devil has devised his own trinity for the end-times. Together with Satan as the unholy god, the Antichrist as the unholy son, the False Prophet will become the unholy trinity spirit. Satan with the Antichrist and the False Prophet are the great deceivers, the great destroyers, and the great dividers for the unsaved people. In the early days angelic Lucifer with third of angels rebelled against God and was defect by archangel Michael. This Satan and third of his angels were cast down from heaven. Satan's description in the Last Days as the "great fiery red dragon," he will pour out his big evil wraths over the whole wide world. Satan the devil has been deceiving people in America and other countries around the world for many thousands years. This Evil One doesn't give up. He was there to deceive Adam and Eve, trying to deceive Jesus in his time, and now he is deceiving in our life journey during this twenty-first century.

My Brothers and Sisters in Christ, this is the last hour for we know for sure that the Antichrist is coming. According to the Bible the Antichrist will be Gentile descent not a Jew. He will be able to perform great signs and wonders, which are false miracles. The book of Revelation relates the Antichrist as of great intelligence and will be politically control of one world government. He will come onto the world stage at a time when there is great chaos. He will sign peace agreements in the Middle East, but they don't last long. Even made agreement with Israel and the Arab nations for making a way for the third temple. Those evil unsaved people on earth will think him as their God, but the truth that he big liar and master deceiver. During the last half of the tribulation period, this lawless one will turn into the evil one. This evil man of sin is the Antichrist, he was given great power from Satan.

> He open his mouth to blaspheme God and slander his name and those live in heaven. He was given power to make war against the saints and to conquer them. He was given authority over every tribe, people, language, and nations. All inhabitants of the earth will worship the beast all whose name have not been written in the book of life belonging to the Lamb.
> (Revelation 13:6-8)

No man or woman will be able to buy or sell anything unless they have the mark of the beast, that of 666, which will be placed on the right hand or on the forehead. At one time in the past several years this was not possible, now with microchips, MRI testing, smart phones, and modern computer technology; all people can be traced anywhere in the world. The Bible states in the end times or last days of this church age, that knowledge shall increase. That time is Now as Big Brother is there watching you with cameras as you are doing your banking or shopping. Be sure that your name is written in the Lamb Book of Life that you will be heaven bound.

> Don't let anyone deceive you in any way, for
> that day will not come until the rebellion
> occurs and the man of lawlessness is revealed,
> the man doomed to destruction.
> He will oppose and will exalt himself over
> everything, proclaiming himself as God.
> The coming of the lawless one is according to
> the working of Satan, displayed in all kinds.
> (2 Thessalonians 2:3-4)

> He open his mouth in blasphemy against God.
> (Revelation 13: 6)

The False Prophet have the ability bring greater deception at this time, causing many on earth to worship the Antichrist. He will be a counterfeit worldwide religious leader, but his religion will be demonic. This evil one will become the Antichrist's economic czar. He will cause evil people receive the mark 666 of the beast on their right hand or on their forehead. He will use his influence to lead people astray with his false miracles. Some prophecy preachers believe that this evil one might be the last Pope as the evil Pope.

He will cause all, both small and great, rich and poor, free and slave to receive a mark on their right hand or on foreheads, and no one may buy or sell except one has the mark of the beast, or the number of his name.
(Revelation 13:16-17)

If anyone has insight, let him calculate the number of the beast, for it is man's number. His number is 666.
(Revelation 13:18)

Antichrist and the False Prophet are the two evil leaders of the Great Tribulation. The Antichrist will be the world political leader and the False Prophet will be the church spiritual leader. The Antichrist will get his power from Satan the devil and the False Prophet get his power from the Antichrist.

IT TAKES TWO, GOD and YOU with our Lord Jesus Christ to fight these three evil ones.

SEVENTEEN

The Great Awakening

Even during the worst of times, God still have mercy on the unsaved ones that did not take the mark 666 of the beast. At this time the Jews will realized that Jesus Christ is their promised Messiah. Many of them went into the caves, and mountains a place known as Pella to hide from danger. Millions of the unsaved people wanting become Christians in order to escape the coming God's many unbelievable wraths. Our Lord Jesus will protect them from the terrible forces of the Antichrist.

> For God did not appoint us to suffer wrath but
> to receive salvation through our Lord Jesus
> Christ.
> (1 Thessalonians 5:9)

It's wonderful that this old world has awesome Loving God. He the same from the beginning of time up to the times of ever and ever more. God is giving those believing unsaved people one more time to change their sinful life for their own salvation. Amazing grace, how sweet the sound for God saving people like them. God of forgiveness and mercy has four ways for their salvation with protection against the three evil ones, they are the following:

The two Witnesses, the 144,000 Jewish Evangelists, the Angels of Everlasting Gospel with the major outpouring of the Holy Spirit.

These are the ones that will bring salvation to those faithful unsaved people during those trouble times—that is if these unsaved people want to change their sinful ways.

Out of these sent by God are the Two Witnesses will serve from Jerusalem with God's truth of forever love. They will preach with the power of God by prophesying and perform great miracles for three and one-half years during the Great Tribulation. They are able to stop the rain during this time causing droughts, turn water into blood, and strike the earth with many plagues.

> The Two Witnesses will serve from Jerusalem as God's mighty witnesses, and they will boldly preach God's truth and perform awesome Loving God miracles. The Two Witnesses walking with the full power of God will come forth prophesying on God's behave to the whole world for 1,260 days, clothed in sackcloth. They are the two olive trees and the two lampstands that stands before the Lord. Anyone tries to harm them, fire will come from their mouth and devours their enemies.

> These men have power to shut up the sky so
> that it will not rain during the time they are
> prophesying, and they have power to turn
> water into blood and to strike the earth with
> every kind of plague as often they want.
> (Revelation 11:3-6)

After complete God's mission the Antichrist will kill the Two Witnesses. Leaving their bodies for three and a half days on Jerusalem' street to be seen worldwide through satellite TV. There will be great celebration and party time by the evil unsaved people for they are happy that the Two Witnesses are dead. God is always in control for He will bring the Two Witnesses come back alive and then God calling them "Come up here for your heavenly home." this cause great fear among the evil unsaved people. Some Bible Christian preachers have disagreed who are the Two Witnesses, that they might be Elijah and Moses. This is because Jesus was there with them at the Transfiguration. While other Bible preachers believe that they might be Elijah and Enoch. These two never experience death for Elijah the man of God was taken up to heaven in a chariot and horses of fire by a mighty whirlwind. While Enoch walk with God for 300 years and then he was no more for God took him away to His presence.

> When the Two Witnesses have finished their
> testimony, the beast will come up from the
> Abyss will attack them and overpower and
> kill them. Their bodies will lie in the street
> of the great city, which is where our Lord was
> crucified. For three and a half days, men from

every people, tribe, language, and nation will glaze on their bodies and refuse them burial. (Revelation 11: 7-9)

After three and half days a breath of life from God entered the Two Witnesses, and they stood up on their feet, and terror struck those who saw them.
Then they heard a loud voice from heaven saying "Come up here." And they went up to heaven in a cloud, while their enemies looked up.
(Revelation 11: 11-12)

The 144,000 Jewish Spiritual Evangelists are men of God, they completely followed and surrendered to the Lord Jesus.

Then I look, and there before me was the Lamb, standing on Mount Zion, and with him 144,000 who had his name and his Father's name written on their foreheads. These are those who did not defile themselves with women, for they kept themselves pure. They follow the Lamb wherever he goes. No lie was found in their mouth, they are blameless. (Revelation 14:1,4-5)

They are the 12,000 each from the twelve tribes of Israel who committed their lives one hundred percent to the Lord. These are the twelve tribes of Israel: Judah, Reuben, Gad, Asher, Naphtali, Manasseh, Simeon, Issachar, Levi, Zebulun, Joseph, and Benjamin. These 144,000 will have the faith of

Jesus as their Savior in this later-day revival for the nation of Israel. God will protect these special people during the wraths for they will have the Seal of the living God on their foreheads. This Seal symbolizes that they belong to God as His Spiritual Evangelist and will be protected from any harm. They will preach the Gospel of our Lord Jesus with the backing of the Holy Spirit. It will become the Greatest Spiritual Awakening Revival of all times. Millions of people will be saved thru out the world for there will not be anything like it again.

> I looked and there before me was a great multitude that no one could count, from every nation, tribe, people, and language.
> (Revelation 7:9)

> Then I looked, and there before me was the Lamb, standing on Mount Zion, and with him 144,000 who had his name and his Father's name written on their foreheads.
> (Revelation 14:1)

During this seven year tribulation period there will be angels judging through-out the earth. They are three Everlasting Angels and they each have a main purpose. These angels will fly in the heaven with the power of the Everlasting Gospel of our Lord Jesus Christ. The first Everlasting Angel has a message to prepare the world for the Gospel of Lord Jesus. The second Everlasting Angel has a message the Fallen sinful Babylon the Great. The third Everlasting Angel has a message of warning the people of the earth not worship the beast.

Then I saw an angel flying in midair, and he had the eternal gospel to proclaim to those on earth, to every nation, tribe, language, and people. He said in a loud voice, "Fear God and give him the glory, because the hour of his judgment has come. Worship him who made the heaven s, the earth, the sea and the springs of water." A second angel followed and said, "Fallen! Fallen is Babylon the Great, which made all the nations drink maddening wine of adulteries." A third angel followed then and said in a loud voice: "If anyone worship the beast and his image and receives his mark on the forehead or on the hand, he, too, will drink of the wine of God's fury, which has been poured full strength into his cup of his wrath. (Revelation 14:6-10)

There will be the time of rebuilding the city of Babylon, which will have greater power than ever. The rebuilding money will come mostly from the oil rich country of Iraq and from the United Nations. This new Babylon will become world capitol city for banking, commerce, many corporations, and shipping. Later it will become evil city with all kind of sins and vice. God will hear from heaven and pour out His judgment against the Harlots of Babylon. The great Babylon, Antichrist empire headquarters, has Fallen.

> Woe! Woe, O great city, O Babylon, city of power!
> In one hour your doom will come!
> (Revelation18:10)

The Holy Spirit will still be very active on earth, convicting people of their sins and drawing them nearer to the Lord. There will be a Great Revival or better known as The Greatest Awakening during the Great Tribulation period with the backing of the Holy Spirit. This last Great Awakening is for all the people who want to be born again or saved for their salvation. They are the ones who did not take the mark 666 of the beast.

God and our Lord Jesus Christ, which is our Savior, are always in control. The Bible states that the last sign of the end times or the last days the Gospel of our Lord will be preached to all the people around the world.

> And this gospel of the kingdom will be preached in the whole world as a testimony to all nations, and then the end will come. (Matthew 24:14)

At the end of this whole wide world Greatest Spiritual Awakening or the Great Revival of all times on earth which is the ending of seven years of Tribulation. The 144,00 are called up to heaven with much joy in their hearts for their revival mission is now complete. Heaven will be wide open of God's blessing with much joy, much music, much praising, and much singing for the Two Witnesses, the 144,000 Evangelists, and the Everlasting Angeles. Because they saw many people come to Christ for their salvation. In heaven the mighty choir of the 144,000 Evangelists are singing a new song with much joy in their hearts.

> I heard a sound from heaven like the roar of rushing waters and like a loud of thunder.

The sound I heard was like of harpist playing their harps. The 144,000 sang a new song before the throne of God. No one could not could learn the song except the 144,000, for they be redeemed from the earth.
(Revelation 14: 2-4)

Many evil people still with hardened hearts will never change. They believe the Antichrist is their only God. The God of heaven has a place for them that of burning hell where they be there ever, and evermore.

The only blessed hope for the world is only for godliness people not like those evil unsaved people who belong to Satan.

The rest of mankind that were not killed by these plagues still did repent of the works of their hands.
(Revelation 9:20)

For the grace of God that brings salvation as appeared to all men. It teaches us to say "No" to ungodliness and worldly passions and to live self- controlled, upright and godly lives in this present age, while we wait for the blessed hope—the glorious appearing of our great God and Savior, Jesus Christ, who give himself for us to redeem us from wickedness and to purity for himself a people that are his very own, eager to do what is good. These then, are the things you should teach. Encourage and

rebuke with all authority. Do not let anyone despise you.
(Titus 2: 11-15)

IT TAKES TWO, GOD and YOU with the Two Witnesses, 144,000 Evangelists, and the Three Everlasting Angels with the backing of the Holy Spirit.

EIGHTEEN

Jesus Second Coming

We saw the four horsemen of the Apocalypse, Satan the devil, the Antichrist the beast, and the False Prophet spreading fear and horror across the world during those seven years of the Tribulation into the terrible Great Tribulation. Now there is another horseman coming from the Heaven of heavens with all His Saints. It's the Second Coming of our Lord Jesus Christ for the Son of Man will come from the heavenly sky with glory and great power.

> At that time, the sign of the Son of Man will appear in the sky, and the nations of the earth will mourn.
> They will see the Son of Man coming on the clouds of the sky, with power and great glory. And he will send his angels with a loud trumpet call, and they will gather his elect from the four winds, from one end of the heavens to the other.

Matthew 24:30-31)

At that time they will see the Son of Man
coming in a cloud with power and great
glory. When these things begin take place,
stand up and lift up your heads, because your
redemption is drawing near.
(Luke 21:27-28)

Just as man is destined to die once, and after
that to face judgment, so Christ was sacrificed
once to take away the sins of many people; and
he will appear a second time, not bear sins, but
to bring salvation to those are waiting for him.
(Hebrews 9:27-28)

Look, he is coming with the clouds, and every eye
will see him, even those who pierced him; and all
the people of earth will mourn because of him.
(Revelation 1:7)

For John saw Heaven open up, the one riding on the big
white horse is our Lord Jesus Christ. His eyes are like blazing
fire, and on his head are many crowns. He is the King of all
kings and the Lord of all lords. He is called Faithful and True.
Throughout the ages there was talk that Jesus was gentle, meek,
and mild. Now he is coming to judge the whole wide world with
a sword out of his mouth, for His sword is the Word of God.

These will be exciting time for the people that are born
again. We will be part of God's heavenly vast army as His
Saints, all riding together on our big white horses in battle
with our Lord Jesus all being dress in clean fine white linen.

He will take down the evil unsaved people of the world and the three Evil Ones of the earth. These evil ones of sins are Satan, Antichrist the beast, and the False Prophet.

The results of this great and last calling from God is the Battle of Armageddon. The final results of this most dramatic and last battle is that the blood of the evil unsaved dead will come up to the horse bridle of 200 miles. It takes place in the northern part of Israel all the way to the southern part, an area approximately several miles long and wide. Most of the famous battles of Israel have accord in the Valley of Megiddo. This valley has seen many battles and wars over thousands of years. Now it's the final battle, it will be the War of all wars with all together army of two-hundred million evil men. Jesus will come through the clouds with great glory and power. He will descend to earth with his all Saints army. Every eye shall see Him as He stand on the Mount of Olives to fight against all those evil nations. Out of his mouth like a sharp two-edge sword which to strike down the nations of the world. The two-hundred million army of the Antichrist and the False Prophet will be destroyed in a few seconds. He has on His robe and thigh a name written in the words. KING OF KINGS AND LORD OF LORDS.

> Then the Lord will go out and fight against those nations, as he fights on a day. On that day his feet will stand on the Mount of Olives, east of Jerusalem, and the Mount of Olives will be split onto from east to west forming a great valley, with half mountain moving north and half moving south.
> (Zechariah 14:3-4)

This is the plague with which the lord will strike all the nations that fought against Jerusalem.

Their flesh will rot while they are standing on their feet, their eyes will rot in their sockets, and their tongues will rot in their mouth.
(Zechariah 14:12)

See, the Lord cometh with ten thousand of his saints.
(Jude 1:14)

I saw heaven standing open and there before me was a white horse whose rider called Faithful and True. with justice he judges and makes war.
(Revelation 19:11)

Now out of His mouth comes a sharp sword, which strikes down the nations. He will rule them with an iron scepter. He treads the winepress of the fury of the wrath God Almighty.

On his robe and on his thigh has his name written:

King of Kings and Lord of Lords.
(Revelation 19:15-16)

Then I saw the beast and the kings of the earth and their armies gathered together to make war against the rider on the horse and his army.
(Revelation 19:19-21)

DON W. ROBERTSON

Next an angel of God will cry out in a loud voice for all the birds to come to the great supper, so that they can eat the flesh of the evil unsaved dead. At that time the Antichrist and the False Prophet are thrown alive into the lake of burning living hell for evermore. Satan the devil is cast into the bottomless pit of Abyss with locked chain and be sealed for one thousand years.

> And I saw an angel standing in the sun, who cried in a loud voice to all the birds flying in midair, Come, gather together for the great supper of God. So that you may eat the flesh of kings, generals, and mighty men, of horses and their riders, and the flesh of all people, free and slave, small and great.
> (Revelation 19:17-18)

> But the beast was captured, and with him the false prophet who had performed the miraculous signs on his behalf. With these signs he had deluded those who had received the mark of the beast and worshiped his image. The two of them were thrown alive into the fiery lake of burning sulfur. The rest of them were killed with the sword that came out the mouth of the rider on the horse, and all the birds gorged themselves on their flesh.
> ¶ (Revelation 19:20-21)

> And I saw an angel coming down out of heaven, having the key to the to the Abyss and holding in his hand a great chain. He seized

the dragon, who is the devil, or Satan, and
bounded him for a thousand years. That keep
him from deceiving the nations anymore until
the thousand years were ended.
After that, he must be set free for a short time.
(Revelation 20:1-3)

At that time, the sun will become black and the moon
will turn blood red. There will be a brief time period where
there be no light from the moon, stars, and the sun. A great
earthquake will divide the Mount of Olives to make a water
port out of Jerusalem. These events will occur during the
final day of the Great Tribulation which is the worst of all
times.

On that day there will be no light. It will be
a unique day, without daytime or nighttime
there be no light.
(Zechariah 14:6-7)

IT TAKES TWO, GOD and YOU with THE KING of
KINGS and LORD of LORDS.

NINETEEN

The Millennium

The Millennium will be one thousand year ruled by Jesus Christ from Jerusalem on earth. It will be the new paradise world, like the Garden of Eden, for all those born again faithful Christians, all done with God's blessing and glory from the kingdom of heaven. Being a total living peaceful world with no more wars, without health concerns by living longer, babies being born, and seeing playful children. There will be those outstanding praising time with greater joy in the Lord with the Angels, and all the Saints. It be the best relaxation time, great worship times, and those special times for those daily forever talks and longer walks with our Lord Jesus. The gates of Jerusalem, the Holy City of Love, will always be open, just come as you are.

> The nations in the world will beat their swords into plowshares, and their spears into pruning hooks. Nations shall not take up swords

against nations, nor will they train for war anymore.
(Isaiah 2:4)

They rejoice before You according to the joy of the harvest.
(Isaiah 9:3)

The wolf will live with the lamb, the leopard ill lie down with the goat, the calk and the a lion and the yearling together; and a child will lead them. They will neither harm or destroy on all my holy mountain, for the earth will be full of the knowledge of the Lord as the water cover the sea.
(Isaiah 11:6, 11:9)

He will judge between many peoples and will settle disputes or strong nations far and wide. They will beat their swords into plowshares and their spears into pruning hooks. Nations will not take up sword against nations, nor will they train for war anymore. Every man will sit under his own vine and under his own fig tree, and no one will make them afraid, for the Lord has spoken. Will walk in the name of the Lord our God for ever and ever.
(Micah 4:3-5)

I saw thrones on which were seated those who had been given authority to judge.

> And I saw the souls of those who had been
> beheaded because of their testimony for Jesus
> and because of the word of God.
> They had not worship the beast or his image
> and had not received his mark on their
> foreheads or on their hands. They came to life
> and reigned with Christ for a thousand years.
> (Revelation 20:4)

During those glory millennium times women will have children, and in turn, their children will have children. Those children and their children may not have the same kind of faith as their parents and grandparents. It will be different kind of sin during this millennium time. It will not be same temptation of Satan, this kind of sin during this millennium time will be one's own nature. At that time Ole Satan the devil, the evil one, will be released from the bottomless pit and will take advantage of those unfaithful people for the last time. The devil will go out to deceive the nations in the four corners of the earth to gather them for the final battle. It is unbelievable how those people gave up the good life in a place more like the Garden of Eden for their future living lake of burning hell. Satan with his evil unfaithful followers which are in the number too many to count will march toward Jerusalem. Our Heavenly Father has other plans for all of them. It will be fire coming down from heaven and devouring those unfaithful sinners. Satan the devil that deceived people for thousands of years will be thrown into the lake of burning hell. The same place where the Antichrist and the False Prophet had been thrown over one thousand years ago. They will be tormented day and night forever and ever-more. This will be the final end of the three evil ones, that of the Satan the devil, the Antichrist the beast, and the False Prophet. The only people left on the earth after this great last terrible event will be all the faithful true Christians.

> When the thousand years are over, Satan will be release from his prison and go out to deceive the nations in the four corners of the earth—Gog and Magog to gather them for battle.
> In number they are like the sands on the seashore. They march across the breadth of the earth and surround the camp of God's people, the city he loves. But fire came down from heaven and devoured them. And the devil that deceived them, was thrown into the lake of burning sulfur, where the beast and the false prophet had been thrown. They will be tormented day and night for ever.
> (Revelation 20:7-10)

The Lamb's Book of Life have the names of all faithful people, they are the born again, known to God as destined for eternal life in heaven. This is the book of righteous, you don't want your name blotted out by belonging to Satan or the beast. We are thankful for the Savior of the world that provided our salvation with eternal life.

> May they be blotted out of the book of life and not be listed with the righteous.
> (Psalm 69:28)

DON W. ROBERTSON

The very definition of our Lord is this: "God is love."
(1John 4:8)

He who overcomes will, be dress in white. I will never blot out his name from the book of life, but will knowledge his name before my Father and his angels.
(Revelation 3: 4-5)

Nothing impure will enter it, nor anyone who does what is shameful or deceitful, but only those whose name are written in the Lamb's Book of life.
(Revelation 21:27)

At the end of the Millennium, all the wicked dead unfaithful people from the time of Adam and Eve will be resurrected from Hades for that final sad judgment time being judge by God of the Great White Throne Judgement for those receiving that second death into torment of firing hell.

Then I saw a great white throne and him who was seated on it, And I saw the dead, great and small, standing before the throne, and books were opened.
Another book was opened, which is the book of life.
The dead was judged according to what they have done as is recorded in the books. The sea gave up the dead that were in it, and death and Hades gave up the dead that were in them, and

each person was judged according to what he had done. Then death and Hades were thrown into the lake of fire. The lake of fire is the second death.

If anyone name was not found written in the book of life, he was thrown in the lake of fire. (Revelation 20: 11-15)

IT TAKES TWO, GOD and YOU will be living in the Millennium with our Lord Jesus

TWENTY

The New Jerusalem

There coming a glorious day when the kingdom of this world will become the kingdom of our Lord Jesus Christ, He is King of kings and the Lord of lords.

After the events of the end-times and the Millennium of one thousand years, the current heaven and earth will pass away and be replaced with the new heaven and the new earth. It's on the new earth where the New Jerusalem, the Heavenly Holy City, will be coming down from the third heaven. The New Jerusalem will be free from death, evil, sickness, sin, suffering, and rumors of wars. It will be a place where we will dwell with our glorified new bodies. Our bodies will be like Christ's glorified resurrected body and we will be glorious, imperishable, and powerful. All God's children will live in a new sin-free physical bodies. Thankful for all those blessings from our Savior for our glorified perfect body with praising of glory and rejoicing to the Son of God. There always be gladness time with rejoicing and praising with our Lord

Jesus. Again and time again we will be hearing the heavenly angels choir singing by rejoicing to our Lord Jesus Christ.

The Bible opens and ended with basically the same type of setting. The first chapter of Genesis is God's creation of the heavens, earth, and preparing of man and woman. The last part of the Bible in the book of Revelation, that our Heavenly God will create the new heaven, the new earth, and those faithful Christians with their glorious bodies. Next seeing the Holy City, The New Jerusalem, coming down out of the Heaven of all heavens as beautiful dressed as a new bride for her husband all done in the glory of God. These are special creations from heaven being special made by our God for all the believing faithful Christians. The sound of crying and weeping will be heard no-more. We will be living on this new earth by seeing the new heaven and living in the Holy City of rightness, the New Jerusalem, with our Lord Jesus for evermore.

> Behold, I will create a new heaven and new earth. The former things will not remember, nor will they come to mind.
> But be glad and rejoice forever in what I create, for I will create Jerusalem to be a delight and its people a joy. I will rejoice over Jerusalem and take delight in my people, The sound of weeping and of crying will be heard in it no more.
> (Isaiah 65: 17-19)

> That day will bring about the destruction of the heavens by fire, and the elements will melt

by the heat. But in keeping with his promise
we are looking forward to a new heaven and a
new earth, the home of rightness.
(2 Peter 3: 12-13)

Then I saw a new heaven and a new earth, for
the first heaven and the first earth had passed
away, and there was no longer any sea.
I saw the Holly City, the Jerusalem, coming
down out heaven from God, prepared as a
bride, beautifully dressed for her husband.
And I heard a loud voice from the throne
saying, "Now the dwelling of God is with men,
and he will live with them. They will be his
people, and God himself will be with them
and be their God. There will be no more death
or mourning or crying or pain, for the old
order of things has passed away."
(Revelation 21:1-4)

He who overcomes will inherit all this, and I
will be his God and he my son.
(Revelation 21:7)

John describes our eternal home of the New Jerusalem
as a city that is foursquare of 1,400 cubits-miles. That's 1,400
miles high, that's 1,400 miles long, that's 1,400 miles wide.
It will shine with the glory of God and its brilliance be like
a very precious jewel, like a jasper clear as crystals. With its
twelve gates always be open and made of pearls which are
written the names of the twelve tribes of Israel. The wall of

the city has twelve foundations written with the names of the twelve apostles of the Lamb. This city of God will not need the lamp light, the moon light, and the sun light. The light will come from our Lord's glory. Living in this Holy City of God is only for those people whose names are written in the Lamb's Book of Life.

> The city does not need the sun or the moon to
> shine on it, for the glory of God gives it light,
> and the Lamb is the lamp.
> The nations will walk by its light and the kings
> of the earth will bring their splendor unto it.
> On no day will the gates will be shut.
> (Revelation 21: 23-25)

There is the river of life, that is clear as crystal flowing from the throne of God and of the Lamb. Which is located in the middle the great street of the Glorious Holy City. On each side of the river of life, stood the tree of life, bearing twelve crops of fruit, yielding its fruit every month.

> God show John the river of life on each side of
> the river stood the tree of life, bearing twelve
> crops of fruit, yielding the fruit every month.
> The leaves of the tree are the healing of the
> nations.
> (Revelation 22:1-2)

Thank you Lord Jesus Christ for our salvation. We are the faithful born again or saved people, that have our name written in the Lambs Book of Life. Gratitude to the Lord for our Christian citizenship be living in the Holy City of Love.

That make it the time for our Blessing Time, our Hallelujah Time, and our Praising Time in the Lord Jesus Christ.

Lord Jesus will come in the fullness of His glory to receive into His glory those who believe in Him. The believers in their glorified bodies will be like our Lord Jesus in His glorified body at His same age of 33. The people will be free to come and go into the Holy City of New Jerusalem. All God's children will have our daily talking and walking with our Lord Jesus. What a glorious time that will be— time for living with our Lord Jesus forever and ever more with no end. Yes, most important of all we will see Him face to face. There will be greater Faith, Hope, Joy, and more Love than ever. Being children of God we will be singing and shouting in Victory for it will become a glorious happy time with Victory in Jesus. Hallelujah, being our Morning Star.

> How great is the love of the Father has lavished on us, that we should be called children of God! And that is what we are! But we know that when Christ appears, we shall be like Him, for we shall see him as he is. Everyone who have this hope in him purify himself as he is pure. (1 John 3: 1-3)

> Behold, I am coming soon! My reward is with me, and I will give to everyone according to what he has done. I am the Alpha and the Omega, the First and the Last, the Beginning and the Ending. Blessed are those who wash their robes, that they may have the right to the tree of life and go through the gates into the

city. I Jesus have sent my angel to give you this testimony for the churches. I am the Root and the Offspring of David and the Morning Star. (Revelation 22: 12-13, 16)

I warn everyone who hears the words of the prophecy of this book: If anyone adds anything to them, God will add to him the plagues described in this book. And if anyone takes any words away from this book of prophecy, God will take away from him his share in the tree of life and in the holy city, which is describe in this book.
(Revelation 22: 18-19)

"Yes, I am coming."
Amen, Come, Lord Jesus
The grace of the Lord Jesus be with God's people. Amen.
(Revelation 22:20-21)

IT TAKE TWO, GOD and YOU with JESUS living in the new heaven. the new earth, and the New Jerusalem.

TWENTY-ONE

Praying Time

In this final chapter, I will be praying for you, your family, our great America and their leaders, and for our brave military and veterans. It's the home with both faithful father and mother—that forms a good family relationship. That is one man as the husband and one woman as his wife. Being faithful parent is a big challenge, a privilege, and bigger responsibility. Parents should always be the backbone and the heartbeat providing good Christian relationship with their children and grandchildren. This will become more real by family togetherness for those daily reading and study Bible times, those daily prayer times, mostly for those faithful family times going to church each week, and doing those great happy times being together as a family. When faithful parents are there helping their children to live the ways of our Heavenly Father, this in-turned created a faithful, powerful, and stronger America. For those marriage or family needs just ask in Jesus's name for He will give you and your family the following: Faith, Health, Hope, Love, Salvation, Wealth, and Wisdom, all these will last a life time.

The faithful people of America been praying for our Country the United States of America since the early 1600's, the day when the Pilgrims got off those wooden ships and got on their knees in prayer for their new world. Prayers have been answer from the years of the First President George Washington of the 1700's with greater prayers for all those future presidents of the twenty-first century. Let's pray that our Heavenly Father will bless and heal our country again. Our country need God's blessing for greater leadership in the business world and the leaders on Capitol Hill, that they have the Love of Jesus and the wisdom of Solomon. We are so blessed that God providing our Forty-fifth President Donald J. Trump and his Vice President Mike Pence and their faithful Cabinet team members the knowledge, understanding, and wisdom of leading our America to economic greatness again. They were there even during good or hard times as the situation with COVID-19 and later for on time delivery working vaccines.

Members of the U.S. Congress must work together with any America's President, Vice President and their Cabinet team. Also, there must be better relationship between any president and members of U.S. Congress with the nine judges of U.S. Supreme Court and those federal judges of having a better conservative justice system. Its' time put an end of this "do nothing congress" regarding with the division between the D Party and the GOP. There must be more teamwork within the member of Congress for a greater country having a powerful military. For those members of Congress on Capitol Hill it's time for you to roll up your shirt sleeves, get your hands dirty, and go back to work. All these will make bigger difference for our country going forward with greatness. We must pray for faithful and lasting relationship between America with Israel, their people, and their Prime Minister.

One of my best experience was the military, served my country for three years in the U.S. Army Finance. Took my GI Bill got a BS Accounting Degree from Ball State University located in Muncie, Indiana. Let us pray each day for our brave and proud active military men and women and those veterans that fought for our America giving us so much freedom and liberty. May God Bless you all for serving your America that we all love. All the people of America must take time to thank these fighting warriors and their proud family.

I wish to leave everyone with these final words:

Grow in the grace and knowledge of our Lord Jesus Christ for being our Salvation Savior. Let's make every day of your life as it is Easter Sunday, for the risen Christ as our Salvation Savior for coming into our heart and life. Go to church every Sunday like it's Christmas with your family and friends. Because Jesus Christ, the King of kings and the Lord of lords came from heaven to be born as a baby, later become the Savior of the world. After three years of His ministry, He was beaten and died on a wooden cross for me and you. Because of His resurrection body, we are born again or saved with the free gift of our Salvation thru our faith and by God's grace and Jesus's love that our sins are forgiven and forgotten forever.

To him be glory both now and forever! Amen.
(2 Peter 3:18)

WHERE HAVE ALL THOSE YEARS WENT

Most people of those golden years have said those same words several times. "Where have all those years went, time goes by so fast?" We are living today, gone tomorrow. Along life journey there will be both good and hard times facing everyone. Just remember these words: As always, the roses will bloom again during your life journey. God has a plan and purpose for your life, make the most of your life each day for our Lord Jesus. Most of us have lived the good life by believing the Holy Bible as Word of our Heavenly Father with the Living Love of our Lord Jesus. Most important of all, God want everyone have their salvation being heaven bound that you will have that living love and forever peace in your body, heart, life, mind, and soul.

Start each morning with a cup of C.O.F.F.E.E, that is:

CHRIST- OFFER- FOEGIVENESS- for- EVERYONE- EVERYWHERE.

Have a Cup of coffee with Lord Jesus Christ.

Keep looking up, be ready, and keep on watching for that day when Jesus will be coming in the clouds for His Church. It's not about how long we live, but how we live, and how we love. Always leave a happy trail of your life by showing your faith, your kindness, and your love. Be sure that everyone will be much happier because you have passed in their life journey. God's Blessing to my love ones of the many years yet to come by having Lord Jesus Christ as your Salvation Savior and Shepherd.

The Lord is my shepherd, I shall not be in want.

He makes me lie down in green pastures,
He leads me beside quite waters, he restores my
soul. He guides me in paths of righteousness
for his name sake. Even though I walk through
the valley of the shallow of death, I will fear
no evil, for you are with m your rod and your
staff, they comfort me. You prepare a table
before me in the presence of my enemies.
You anoint my head with oil; my cup overflows.
Surely goodness and love will follow me all the
days of my life, and I will dwell in the house of
the Lord forever.
(Psalm 23: 1-6)

Sing to the Lord a new song for He has done many outstanding things for you and your family. The good news is that you and your family are born again, saved by your Faith thru the Grace and Love of our Lord Jesus Christ. After your salvation, the most important thing that you and your family are on your way to your heavenly home. Be thankful for all the blessings with promise of love that was given to you. The Lord Jesus will be there in heaven with open arms, saying to you all "Will done my faithful Sons and Daughters, welcome to your Heavenly Home."

IT TAKES TWO, GOD and YOU always keep looking up for the Lord Jesus is coming soon.

KEEP LOOKING UP

Wanting to share regarding our small churches across our America, many of them are closing their doors for good. Several of these small churches have only twenty-five people that is more or less coming for Sunday worship. Some ministers have two or three small churches each Sunday or weekly services to share the Word of God with the Love of our Lord Jesus. There is one small church that stand out because of this one preacher Rev. Frank Bunn and his wife Mary Ellen Bunn, they came out their retirement years reopen the New Maysville Community Church that been closed over four years. Their Heavenly Father had a newer plan and purpose for them and it's been a Blessing of all blessing.

While we were still in our mother's womb, our Heavenly Father has a plan or purpose for our life journey by having our heavenly home. It's up to each person for that purpose during their life journey by taking the narrow road of God's greater light for that future heavenly home or take the wider road of Satan's darkness leading to that burning fire of hell. My Heavenly Father has blessed me all my life, more so in my "Golden Years." My extra purpose in this life journey to informed my dear Brothers and Sisters in Christ of what our Lord want you to learn regarding the vanishing small churches and the vanishing small communities and towns across America.

This write-up story is in the memory of Rev. Frank Bunn and his wife Mary Ellen Bunn. Preacher Frank graduated from the Moody Bible Institute of Chicago. He preached over fifty years mostly small churches in both Hendricks County and Putnam County of Middle-Indiana. After his retirement with his wife for their "golden years," they settle down on their small farm in Putnam County, Indiana. As Paul Harvey would say it on national radio years ago "Now for the rest of the story." What a story it turned out, let's turn that radio on for the final chapters of this Hoosier Preacher and his wife of that newer God's purpose for them.

One day retired Preacher Frank drove his car into the nearby small farming community of New Maysville, Putnam County, Indiana and saw this run-down old white frame church all grown-up in weeds. At that time this old timer church been without both life and light for over four years. He stopped his car and got out to look this church over. Lady across the road saw him and she asked him "Are you a preacher, I want be saved." That start a newer Heavenly Father calling for him to rebuild and restart this old church and start preaching again. Those four words "I want be saved" charged up his heart for his newer God's calling to preach again. Local faithful men came to help, roll up their sleeves, and got those hands dirty by rebuilding the inside of this old church. The final results what outstanding job with rest room, design wooden cross, new carpet, pews, windows, new roof, and paint inside and outside. Several years later building larger add-on for fellowship and class rooms.

Maybe at one time in the many past years ago this little white frame church would seem like The Little Church in the Wild Wood, not any more. On Easter Sunday April 3, 1988, they answered the call to Resurrect the New Maysville Community Church. Almost year later with memorial services to dedicated to those founding twenty-four men and women of the first Lord's day in July 1839 of 150 years ago for this little Church in God's glory. We are thankful for those faithful pastors and preachers sharing the Gospel in those small churches in the communities and towns across America. They became the heartbeat of our America for sharing the Word of God with the Love of our Lord Jesus.

At this time will share parts of two poems for those preachers in those smaller churches:

"The Preacher."

> He' just a smalltime Country Preacher
> And the call was loud and clear
> Preach the Gospel to everyone
> But he knowns the Lord wants him here.
> But he's no less a Man of God.

"Little Churches"

> God bless the little churches-
> Tucked into a clearing in the woods,
> Standing weather beaten on a lonely prairie,
> Or sitting sedately on a corner of a quiet village street.
> God's blessing must fall on all the little churches.

Our Heavenly Father had a plan or purpose for each person, it must be true for each pastor or preacher by taken that plan and purpose for their life journey become God's Shepherd. That was true with preachers like Billy Sunday, Billy Graham, and those pastors of those little churches in the wild wood. This was true by those founding men and women of 1839, they had greater dreams and vision for those plans and purpose of reaching out with the Holy Word of God and have Jesus Christ being the chief cornerstone of this country church. From year 1988 into this twenty-first century Preacher Frank Bunn with his wife, Mary Ellen, have carry out their ministry for the New Maysville Community

Church for greater newer plan and purpose by taken the Bible as the only rule of faith and practice. Because of Preacher Frank passing away few years ago, this church has a new Shephard for the Savior with Preacher Larry Edwards and his wife Glena for that forward greater purpose. Is the time for our Heavenly Father's having that Wake-Up Calling for a whole wide world greater revival before the near coming Rapture? For it only takes one preacher or one little church in the wildwood to rekindle that greater revival fire.

Putnam County, Indiana was organized by an Act of the General Assembly, approved December 1821, was named in honor of Revolutionary War General Israel Putnam. Those Early Settlers of the New Maysville Community came from the states of Kentucky, North Carolina, and Virginia. The town of New Maysville was founded in June 1832, named by Richard Biddle being one of those early settlers. At one time the population of this farming community was over 175 people. During those first 150 years, there were three different churches, school house, blacksmith, saw mill, livery stable, and other small business. Also, four general stores consisting barber shop and post office. One of those old general stores was the oldest general store in Indiana. I been in that old general store few times several years ago to look around and buying five cent bottle of coke on my way to the local main cemetery.

Now this small farming community is down maybe twenty some homes, no stores, no school house, one church, and nearby two cemeteries. People come and just moved away for better lifestyle in bigger towns and cities. Many of these small communities, towns, and villages that are located off the beaten paths from bigger highways are slowly blowing in the wind. Even those pop and mom stores are going out of business, never return again. I enjoy getting off the busy interstate highways and drive thru those small towns. Driving down main street seeing those nice older homes, next going into the main part of town seeing the court house and those business places around the town square. It's someone, Sweet Home Town. Yes, just like my childhood home town during those school years there in Danville, Indiana for it's still someone Sweet Home Town.

The year 2003 my second wife and myself were on our way from Tennessee to Danville for my1953 high school class mate's fifty-year celebration dinner and reunion that Saturday night. The very next day we were on our way to Turkey Run State Park for my cousin family dinner reunion. I told my wife will turn here at Groveland and take you to the New Maysville cemetery where my mother, her sister, their parents, grant parents, and the great-grand parents are buried. When we came into this small community of New Maysville, we past the only church in town on our way to the main cemetery. Across the road from that bigger cemetery is the older cemetery where those Early Settlers are buried. When we travel anywhere always go to some church for Sunday worship, so we stop that Sunday morning services at this small country church.

What a welcome we received, told the preacher and his wife that we just came from the cemetery on the way to Turkey Run State Park for my family dinner-reunion at the Inn. This old time preacher man had great sermon for he told it as it is. This Man of God close his sermon with these three words "Keep Looking Up. Every year or different times when we made those Indiana trips always stop for Sunday services at the New Maysville Community Church. On the way back to our home we always visit with Preacher Frank and Mary Ellen at their lovely farm house. They sharing their ministry over the years including some history of New Maysville. In-turn I share about my New Maysville family roots being born in farm house near his church and that I went the first grade at the local New Maysville school. The next day from those wonderful trips, Mary Ellen would phone us make sure "Us kids got home safe." It made us feel really good being back home again in Indiana with our new church family. Thank you both Preacher Frank and Mary Ellen being faithful children of God and being our special friends.

This old time preacher man was still preaching the Word of God and the Love of Jesus for this country church up-to the age of almost eighty-nine with the final words of each sermon "Keep Looking Up. Then the good Lord took him home, couple years later his wife joined him being together forever. Keep looking up for the Rapture is coming very soon. Until, we will meet again in Heaven.

Just like Preacher Frank Bunn and his wife, we will be singing that that gospel song: "I'll will fly away."

> Some glad morning, when life is over, I'll fly away to a home on God's celestial shore, I'll fly away I'll fly away, O' glory, I'll fly away, when I die in the morning, Hallelujah, by and by, I'll fly away.

Somewhere in America there the most faithful Man of God with the Holy Bible in his hand praying for a Breakthrough fire-up Holy Spirit Revival. His faithful church maybe like the Tittle Church in the Wildwood or the New Maysville Community Church. Faithful Brothers and Sisters in Christ lets be in prayer in Jesus name that the Holy Spirit will rekindle those revival fires like a wild whirlwind for that whole wide world revival. With God Blessing with the Holy Spirit will there be another Great Awakening like the ones in past years? Let's look at those pass-years Great Awakenings.

- The First Great Awakening was from 1735 to 1740 led by Jonathan Edwards and evangelist George Whitefield. Our America as a nation was spiritual born again because of this awakening.
- The Second Great Awakening happened from 1790's to around 1840. It was led by Charles Finney as wilderness camp meetings or tent revivals for the western frontier people.
- The Third Great Awakening was from around 1857 to 1859, at a prayer meeting led by preacher Jeremiah Lanphier. Because of fear and panic caused by the New York stock market crash and depression, this became stronger spiritual awakening hundreds of thousands people going to church and being born again.
- The Fourth Great Awakening of the 1960s and 1970s led by Pastor Chuck Smith and his church. It was known the Jesus Movement consisting mostly young people known as hippies with their loud music.

America has turn back on God, but God has not turn His back on America. Will there be Fifth Great Awakening before the Rapture of His Church during this twenty-first century? With increased faith the Heavenly Father will answer.

COME SOON LORD JESUS.

The greatest of all them will be the GREAT AWAKENING led by the Two Witnesses and the 144,00 Evangelists with the backing of the Holy Spirit.

REFERENCE

IT TAKES TWO, GOD and YOU and KEEP LOOKING UP

The words that God gave me to write and the Bible verses taken from NIV Study Bible, New International Version.

Printed in the United States
by Baker & Taylor Publisher Services